BIG BIBLE SCIENCE

Experiment and Explore God's World

ERIN LEE GREEN

CF4•K

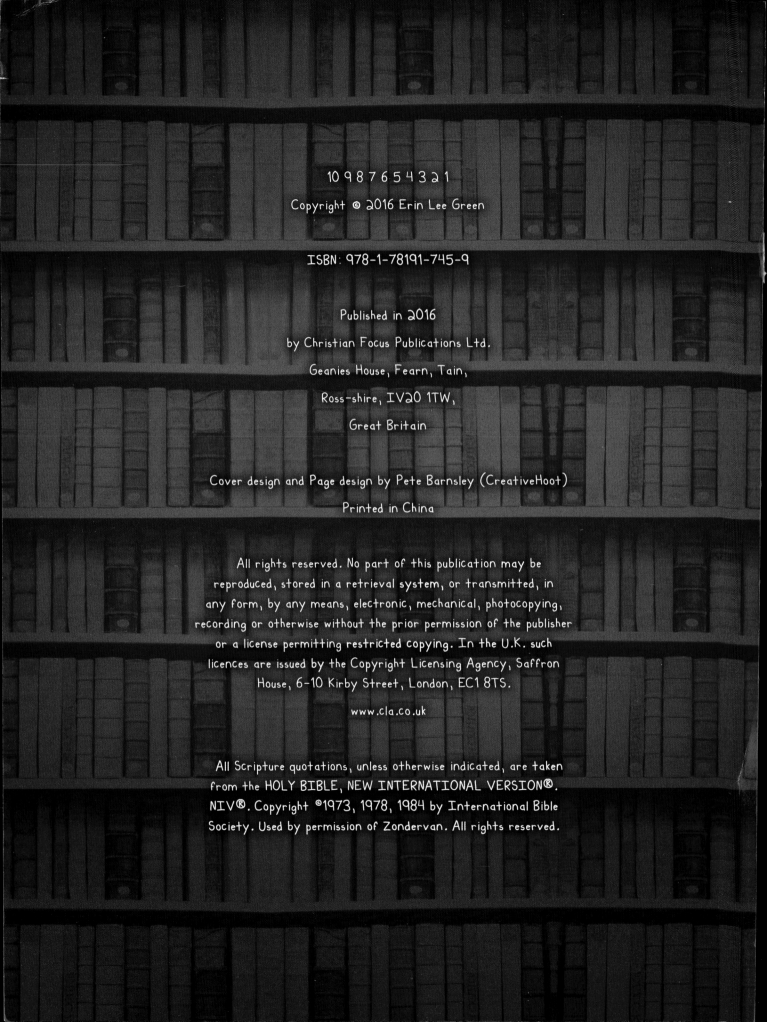

10 9 8 7 6 5 4 3 2 1

Copyright © 2016 Erin Lee Green

ISBN: 978-1-78191-745-9

Published in 2016

by Christian Focus Publications Ltd.

Geanies House, Fearn, Tain,

Ross-shire, IV20 1TW,

Great Britain

Cover design and Page design by Pete Barnsley (CreativeHoot)

Printed in China

CONTENTS:

Introduction 5

How to make the most of every lesson 6

Chapter Components 7

Safety First 8

Miscellaneous 9

Notebooking 11

Gravity 12

Newton's First Law of Motion 15

Newton's Second Law of Motion 19

Newton's Third Law of Motion 23

Coefficient of Friction 27

Static Electricity 30

Acids and Bases 34

Combustion Reactions 38

Plant Requirements 41

Lunar Craters 45

Water Cycle 49

Angle of the Sun's Rays 54

Basic Animal Classification 58

Animal Classification: Zoo Trip 61

Nervous System 64

Muscles 69

Bones 73

Respiratory System 76

Circulatory System 80

Digestive System 84

Urinary System 88

Mini Biographies 91

Some extra activities to accompany this book are available on www.christianfocus.com – just go to the children's books and search for Big Bible Science.

INTRODUCTION:

Each question your child asks is a teaching opportunity. Children are in a constant state of scientific investigation, with astonishing curiosity about the world around them. They naturally have scientific minds and questions. Their senses are bombarded with new experiences. Each time a young student learns a concept, his or her brain creates a neural pathway to integrate this new understanding. When the concept is repeated, the neural pathway is strengthened. The more this pathway is used, the stronger it will become. If it is not used, it can become lost. Every question is an open door to a potential new neural pathway.

God creates young minds to ask questions and seek answers. Ecclesiastes 3:11 reminds us, "He has made everything beautiful in its time. He has also set eternity in the human heart; yet no one can fathom what God has done from beginning to end." God writes His name on everything He creates. Children are designed to seek Him. It is up to teachers and parents to encourage our children to recognize God in the world. Educators should respond to students' questions with warmth and enthusiasm, help them discover, empower them to learn, and lay a firm foundation for a life-long relationship with God. Bringing students to love and worship Christ is the ultimate goal of Christian education. If you can show children God's creation, then you will inevitably bring them closer to Him.

But where to start in a world full of science that outwardly contradicts the Bible? Job 12:7-10 tells us to "ask the animals, and they will teach you, or the birds in the sky, and they will tell you; or speak to the earth, and it will teach you, or let the fish in the sea inform you. Which of all these does not know that the hand of the Lord has done this? In His hand is the life of every creature and the breath of all mankind." Science must be framed by the Bible, especially for the young learner. Although the writers of the Bible did not know about atomic theory or the carbon cycle, they understood that the natural world was God's good creation, a teacher of God's love, greatness, and mystery.

This book is designed to stir the imaginations of students and develop a lasting love for Christ.

The units are fun, interesting, and affirm the biblical worldview of creation.

The units are written to appeal to various ages and learning styles.

Homeschool families will benefit by encouraging older students to elaborate on the experiments, while younger students delight in the simpler activities.

Classroom teachers will enjoy the group activities and games.

Repetition of the various aspects of each unit is critical to form and reinforce new neural pathways and inspire a child to further curiosity.

HOW TO MAKE THE MOST OF EVERY LESSON:

TIMING

In order to enjoy teaching and learning these lessons, try not to rush. Move at a pace that is comfortable to your students. When attention spans wane, come to a stopping place and finish the lesson at another time. Take some time each day for about a week, repeating the stories and activities that hold the children's interest. Write science notebooks, practice memory verses, memorize scientific concepts, encourage further experimentation, and research the students' additional questions.

PRAYER

Begin each lesson with a prayer for God to open the minds of the children, help them concentrate, give the teacher patience, and for everyone to enjoy learning about His creation.

Leading a child to Christ is a blessed responsibility. Pray for your students, and be Spirit led for the right time to invite them to follow Him. Do not be troubled if you think a child is a bit too young or does not fully understand. In Matthew 19:14, "Jesus said, 'Let the little children come to me, and do not hinder them, for the kingdom of heaven belongs to such as these.'" If you have any concerns, seek the Lord and meet with a minister or church elder for advice.

MEMORY VERSE

Each chapter contains a highlighted verse that reinforces the science. Repeat the verse during the science lesson and in the weeks that follow. Memorizing Scripture is important for lasting change in Christians. Memory verses fortify our spirits and prepare us for the future.

Extra activities to accompany this book can be found on this book's page on the website christianfocus.com

BIG BIBLE SCIENCE

CHAPTER COMPONENTS:

OBJECTIVES:

These are simply stated science learning goals. They are for the teacher to get a quick survey of the lesson.

MATERIALS:

Gather and prepare these objects before the lesson, and always have a Bible nearby. Be aware that the anatomy lessons require more time to prepare the materials. The materials are chosen to keep costs low. Most of the items are readily available in the average home or classroom, although a trip to the store will occasionally be necessary. Below is a list of the few special materials that might be more difficult to find.

CHAPTER	MATERIAL	WHERE TO OBTAIN MATERIAL
Newton's Second Law of Motion	Latex exercise band	Sporting goods store, with the exercise equipment.
Combustion Reactions: How a Fire Burns	Baking yeast	Grocery store, baking section.
	Hydrogen Peroxide	Pharmacy, first aid section.
Plant Requirements	Bean seeds	Grocery store, with the dry goods or garden supply store.
Bones	Paper skeleton	Readily available around Halloween. Also can be purchased from internet party supply sites.
All of the anatomy chapters	Sharpie and/or photo marker (any medium soft tip permanent marker will suffice)	Sharpies are available at an office supply store. Photo markers are available where scrapbooking materials are sold.

THE BIG IDEA:

This is a scientific explanation of the lesson. It ties in a biblical perspective and a memory verse as it introduces the lesson. The length of the Big Idea sections vary depending on the complexity of the concepts and the intensity of the Bible lesson. The Big Idea section should be completed before beginning the activities. In many cases, it may be beneficial to review the Big Idea during or after the activities are completed.

ACTIVITIES:

Some activities reinforce the biblical perspective of the lesson, but most are scientific demonstrations, games, and experiments. In most chapters, the order of the activities is not critical.

APPLY IT:

Here you have ideas about how to look for examples of the lesson around the world. Reinforcing the key aspects of the scientific and biblical principles is key for students to retain the information.

GO BEYOND:

This section will challenge more advanced students to think and experiment further.

SAFETY FIRST

The science in this book is quite harmless. However, here are some safety issues that may arise:

FALL RISKS

- Take care when a student or teacher stands on a chair or other elevated position.
- Use teacher/parent discretion regarding child safety on playground equipment.

INJURY RISKS

- Although it is important for the students to have fun while learning, rough housing or misusing equipment is perilous. Manage students' behavior appropriately.
- Use teacher/parent discretion regarding students using sharp objects such as scissors or nails. Keep knives out of children's reach at all times; children should not use knives.
- Do not look directly at the sun. UV destroys cornea cells immediately. Over extended periods of exposure, retinal damage may be permanent. Looking at the sun through binoculars or a telescope is even more damaging as these devices focus the sun's rays. It is completely safe to look at the moon.

CHEMICAL RISKS

- Keep hands away from the face when handling any chemical. Wash hands thoroughly with soap and water after the experiment.
- Vinegar and ammonia are the strongest chemicals used in this book. Safety goggles are a good idea any time these chemicals are called for. Do not breathe the fumes from vinegar or ammonia. If you get these chemicals in the eyes, rinse them immediately with water for at least fifteen minutes. Regarding vinegar, see a doctor if eye irritation persists or gets worse. Regarding ammonia, seek medical attention immediately. If a child drinks vinegar, give him plenty of water to dilute the acid and call a doctor. Do not give him baking soda or induce vomiting. If ammonia contacts the skin, rinse with plenty of water and remove any contaminated clothing.

  MSDS (Material Safety Data Sheet) for vinegar: http://www.cleanersolutions.org/downloads/msds/754/White%20Vinegar%20MSDS.pdf

  MSDS for ammonia: http://www.ciret.co.uk/data-sheets/ammonia.pdf

BURN RISKS

- Never allow a child to operate a stove or hot plate. Keep all cookware handles turned inward. Make sure children are not in your path when you carry hot pots and pans. Take care to keep hands and face clear of any steam, as it can cause severe burns.
- Keep matches and lighters out of reach of children. Always strike matches away from your body. Run smoldering match sticks under water before disposing of them.
- Use vigilant supervision when candles are being utilized. Never leave burning candles unattended.
- Minor burns should be treated as follows:
    - Cool the burn by running it under cool water for 10-15 minutes.
    - Remove any jewelry or tight fitting clothing from the area.
    - Apply lotion, aloe vera, or hydrocortisone cream.
    - See a doctor if the burn covers large areas of the body, large blisters form, or you notice signs of infection.

(Source: The Mayo Clinic)

MISCELLANEOUS

- Wash hands with plenty of soap and warm water after handling meat or bones.
- Children with cochlear implants should not perform any activities involving static electricity.
- The anatomy unit calls for physical contact and touching as various body parts are studied. Make sure all touching is on safe places on the child's body, never on the buttocks, breasts, or groin. Keep clothing ON for all lessons.

If you are a student using this book without an adult, then the exploration aspect of each lesson will be even more fulfilling as you will be free to pursue and experiment on your own terms at your own pace. However, you will not be able to complete many of the activities that require a group of students. In order to make the most of the science, you need at least one partner available whenever an activity calls for assistance. There are a few activities you should not do because they are not safe without an adult.

CHAPTER	ACTIVITIES A STUDENT CAN DO ALONE:	ACTIVITIES THAT REQUIRE ONE OR MORE PARTNERS:	ACTIVITIES A STUDENT CANNOT / SHOULD NOT DO WITHOUT AN ADULT:
Gravity		Which will land first?	
Newton's First Law of Motion	Pennies at Rest New Covenant Alien Headwear	Crazy Driver	
Newton's Second Law of Motion	Both Cars Down a Ramp activities	Acceleration without much Mass Acceleration of Gravity	
Newton's Third Law of Motion	Penny Bump Soda Can Balloon Launch	Sharing Success	
Coefficient of Friction	Slick Pencil Will it Slide? Will it Slide Faster?		
Static Electricity	Charged Balloon Opposites Attract	Wiggle, Slide, and Shock	
Acids and Bases		Acid/Base Taste Test Acid/Base Feel Test	Yucky? Red Cabbage Indicator
Combustion Reactions: How a Fire Burns			Candle Under a Jar Candle Plus CO_2 Under a Jar Candle Plus O_2 Under a Jar
Plant Requirements	Do Plants Need Soil? Do Plants Need Water? Do Plants Need Sun? Do Plants Need Carbon Dioxide?		

CHAPTER	ACTIVITIES A STUDENT CAN DO ALONE:	ACTIVITIES THAT REQUIRE ONE OR MORE PARTNERS:	ACTIVITIES A STUDENT CANNOT / SHOULD NOT DO WITHOUT AN ADULT:
Lunar Craters	Lunar Craters	God Knows You	
Water Cycle	Water Cycle Model Water Cycle Poem God Promises Rain Evaporation and Temperature		Water Usage Conserving Water
Angle of the Sun's Rays	Angle of the Sun's Rays Collecting Data Line Graph Angle of a Flashlight	Stand Still	
Basic Animal Classification	God Created Animals Animal Classification Cards		
Animal Classification Zoo Trip	A Psalm of Praise		Zoo Hunt
Nervous System	Brain Neuron	Do not conform to the pattern of this world Neural Conduction Sending a Message	
Muscles	Muscles Only Pull, Never Push Major Skeletal Muscle Groups	Tug-of-War Voluntary versus Involuntary	
Bones	Major Bones Bones Song What is Inside a Bone	Bones Game	
Respiratory System	Lungs and Trachea	Praise the Lord Act Out Respiration	Structure and Function of the Diaphragm
Circulatory System	The Peace of God Heart Blood Drop	Act out the Parts of the Blood	
Digestive System	Structure and Function of the Digestive System Peristalsis	The "What if" Game	
Urinary System	Parts of the Urinary System	Act Out Urine Components and Nephron Function	

NOTEBOOKING:

It is important to develop good habits of science and encourage sound thinking. A science notebook is a simple way of keeping records of inquiry based observations, experiments, and activities. It is an excellent communication tool for the teacher to access understanding and provide feedback. Notebooks are also an uncomplicated method for integrating math and literacy into a science curriculum. For younger or struggling students, the teacher can model data tables and notebook entries. Older or more advanced students can challenge their minds to organize their own thoughts. A science notebook can be used in multiple scenarios: when the student performs a teacher-guided activity as from this book, observes a natural phenomenon on his/her own, and designs his/her own experiment. A couple of good books to introduce the importance of keeping a science notebook are Galileo's Journal, 1606-1610 by Jeanne Pattenati and Paolo Rui and My Season with Penguins: An Antarctic Journal by Sophie Webb.

GOOD NOTEBOOK HABITS FOR A YOUNG SCIENTIST:

- Use a notebook with stitched binding so pages do not fall out. A simple composition notebook works well. There is no need for the carbon copy type laboratory notebook. Write your full name and the year on the front of the notebook. Write more contact information on the inside of the front cover.

- Use non-water soluble ink. The teacher should use discretion as many children should probably bend this rule and use good graphite pencils, but please do not let them erase. Colored drawings should be done in crayon or colored pencil. Drawings and labeled diagrams are a wonderful way for young children to record data and observations.

- A science notebook is a documentation of facts. It is NOT a diary or record of opinions.

- Starting on the first page, number the fronts of the pages of the notebook. You may need to help your child with this. Devote the first two pages to "Table of Contents," with two columns: one for the name of the experiment, and one for the page number on which it begins. Construct the table of contents as experiments are completed.

- Never tear out a page. You could lose important data and injure your notebook. If a page is skipped, simply draw a single diagonal line across it. If an experiment is concluded before the bottom of a page, draw a diagonal line across the remainder of the page as an indication that it was intentionally left blank.

- Write on the fronts of pages only. Save the backs for sketches, quick notes, photographs, teacher notes, and calculations.

- If you make a mistake, do not erase it, scribble it out, or use White Out. Even if it is a spelling error or a wrong number, just draw a single thin line through the error. So much of the science we now know is correct, was originally thought to be a mistake.

- Use glue, instead of tape, to attach any photographs, data tables, or actual scientific evidence such as leaves or coins.

A science notebook entry for an early elementary age child may contain the following parts:

Page number

Date, written as MM/DD/YY

Title of the experiment

Memory verse

Hypothesis, when appropriate.

Experimental details, data, drawings, observations.

Conclusion: What did you learn?

Further questions: What do you want to learn?

EXAMPLE

Page: 76
10/15/16

Magnets, what will stick?

Proverbs 18:24, A friend sticks closer than a brother.

Material	Hypothesis	Observation
Plastic cup	YES	NO
Nail	Yes	YES
Soccer ball	NO	NO
Penny	YES	NO
Door Hinge	YES	YES

Some metals will stick to a magnet. Why? What makes some metals stick?

GRAVITY

To understand how the pull of gravity affects all objects with the same force.

MATERIALS

1. Approximately 5 balls of varied size and weight (e.g baseball, basketball, golf ball, ping pong ball, marble, etc).

2. Approximately 5 different objects that can fall and hit the ground without fluttering down and without breaking (a piece of paper rolled into a ball shape, stuffed animal, pine cone, rock, penny, wooden stick, etc).

GRAVITY

BIG IDEA

Imagine you are walking through a forest. The light is dim, the ground is uneven, and the trail is unfamiliar. All of a sudden your foot catches on a root and you fall forward onto the ground. Ouch! Have you ever tripped and fallen?

Now, imagine you are walking through the same forest, in the same dim light, on the same uneven ground. But this time you are holding tight to your mother or father's hand. Your foot catches on the same root. What will happen? Will you fall? Of course not; your parent's hand will catch you.

Consider how much stronger the LORD is than your parent.

Psalm 37:23-24 "The LORD makes firm the steps of the one who delights in him; though he may stumble, he will not fall, *for the LORD upholds him with His hand*."

This is an amazing promise! King David wrote this Psalm as an older man. When he was a young man, he sometimes felt frightened and hopeless because he was running for his life from Saul. He probably thought that he would not make it through that very difficult time. However, David delighted in the LORD. God kept him safe from Saul, and eventually David became a great king of Israel. Ask the children to share a time when they were in a bad circumstance, a time when they thought their situation would not end well, but it did. Then ask them to take turns placing their own name in the verse. For instance, Tommy would say, "The LORD upholds *Tommy* with His hand."

God already has a plan for your life. God is always in control. Even when life seems to spin out of control, you can have peace in your heart and hold tight to God's promises. What are some things that God might ask you to do? How could God provide for you?

Hold up a small object; let it fall to the ground. Ask, "Will God let you fall like this?" Hold up the same object. Drop it, but catch it before it hits the ground. Remind the children that "the one who delights in [the LORD]... will not fall, for the LORD upholds him." Ask the children, "Does this mean that you will never get hurt or graze your knee? No. Sometimes bad things happen, but when we trust in the LORD we know that we are safe, even when we die."

God created a very strong force that makes objects fall to the ground. We cannot see this force, but it works around us all of the time. It keeps you in your seat. It keeps the table on the floor. It brings a ball back down when you throw it high. It pulls you to the ground if you trip. Do you know the name of this force? <u>Gravity!</u>

Everything that has mass has gravity. The more mass it has, the more gravity it has. You have mass, so even you have gravity. But since you aren't very big, your gravitational force is not very strong. God made Earth just the right size, so Earth's gravity is perfect for us to live. Earth's gravity holds buildings down, pulls you into your seat, holds the atmosphere in place, and even keeps the moon in its orbit. The acceleration of gravity on Earth is 9.8 meters per second squared ($9.8 \ m/s^2$ or $32 \ ft/s^2$). Since the mass of Earth stays the same, the acceleration of gravity stays the same. It pulls equally on all objects.

What would it be like to live on Earth if we had less gravity? (Things would weigh less, objects would float away, playing baseball would be much harder.) What would it be like to live on Earth if God gave us more gravity? (Things would weigh more, things would fall faster. It would be harder to get out of bed.)

GRAVITY

WHICH WILL LAND FIRST?

1. Carefully climb to a high place, a chair, or a piece of playground equipment from which you can drop these objects while the children watch.

2. Have the kids sit a short distance away so they can clearly see your hands and the floor where the objects will land, but not get hit by any falling objects. (Hint: A soft surface works best as a landing pad, such as grass, mulch, a big pillow, or a blanket).

3. Choose two balls of very different sizes, such as a basketball and a golf ball.

4. Form a hypothesis: Which ball will hit the ground first if they are dropped at the same time?

5. Test the hypothesis by dropping the two balls at the same time so the kids can observe. Make sure that the balls are dropped, not thrown or tossed.

6. You may need to repeat the demonstration several times because their preconceived notion that a larger object will hit the ground first may cloud their observation that both balls land at the same moment.

7. Repeat with two other balls. Continue to repeat steps 3–6 with various balls and objects until the students become convinced that the force of gravity pulls on everything the same.

8. If the children have the coordination to do so safely, allow them to take turns performing the experiment. Remind them to drop objects straight down, not thrown or tossed.

APPLY IT

- Drop various biodegradable objects (such as sticks and rocks) off a bridge into a body of water. The simultaneous splash is very conclusive. Leaves will not work well because they often flutter down, slowing their descent.

- Any time you notice an object falling, repeat the memory verse with your children. Psalm 37:23-24 "The LORD makes firm the steps of the one who delights in Him; though he may stumble, he will not fall, for the LORD upholds him with His hand."

- Study the life of George Müller. (See page 94) How does his walk exemplify Psalm 37:23-24?

GRAVITY

GO BEYOND

Discuss additional examples of gravitational pull:

- The sun's gravity keeps the planets orbiting. Otherwise, they would fly off in a straight line through space.

- The moon (and to a lesser extent, the sun) pulls on the Earth to create the rise and fall of ocean tides every day.

- Why do feathers fall slowly? Because God created them with air resistance. This allows birds to push against the air to fly. If a feather is dropped in a vacuum, where no air is present, it falls like a rock.

Discuss the following scenario.

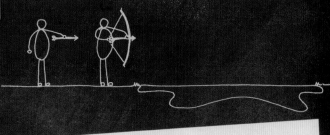

Question:

- One person has a bow and arrow. He holds the bow absolutely straight and aims the arrow level across the water of a calm lake. There is not a target on the lake, the arrow is simply pointing straight out, parallel to the water.

- A second person has an extra arrow, but no bow. He holds the extra arrow in his hand, parallel to the water, next to the other person's bow, at the same height as the first arrow, such that both arrows are the same distance off the ground, but one is strung in the bow while the other is held in a person's hand.

- The bow is pulled back and released, and the extra arrow is dropped at the same moment, not thrown, not tossed, just dropped, such that both arrows are released at the same instant. One arrow flies straight out over the water, while the other just falls to the ground.

- Which will hit first? Or will they hit at the same time?

Answer:

Since the acceleration of gravity is the same for the shot arrow and the dropped arrow, both arrows will land at the same instant, the one dropped straight down and the other out in the lake. Both arrows fell the same distance. The shot arrow simply traveled forward while it fell.

A similar scenario to discuss.

Question:

A group of soldiers waits on the ground for supplies. An airplane has a box to air-drop, and a helicopter has an identical box to air-drop. The airplane and the helicopter are at the same altitude. The airplane flies over the soldiers and drops its box. The helicopter hovers in place over the soldiers and drops its box at the same moment. Which box will hit the ground first?

Answer:

The two boxes will hit the ground at the same time. The box dropped from the airplane will continue to travel horizontally as it falls. But both boxes are pulled to the ground with the same acceleration of gravity, 9.8 m/s².

NEWTON'S
FIRST LAW OF MOTION

Explore how God created objects to move. Memorize and understand that "An object at rest stays at rest, and an object in motion stays in motion with the same speed and in the same direction, unless acted upon by an outside force."

MATERIALS

1. A small ball.

2. Chairs set up to create an imaginary minivan.

3. 10-20 pennies for each student.

4. Sheet of paper for each student.

(Younger students will benefit by using heavier coins and a half sheet of paper).

Sit in a circle around a table or on the floor. While you read the lesson, roll a ball back and forth. Ask the children not to throw or bounce the ball.

BIG IDEA

When God created the earth, He made things that move. Can you think of things that move? (like a humming bird or a race car). Can you show me how you can move?
God also made things that sit still. Can you think of things that sit still? (like a rock or a sleeping cat). Can you show me how you can be at rest?

In the Bible we read about some people who did not believe in Jesus Christ. They stayed the same. They did not move. They did not accept Jesus Christ. They did not change. Others did accept Jesus and Jesus transformed their lives. In Luke 19:1-10 the Bible tells us a story about a man named Zacchaeus. Listen carefully to find out if he was moved by Jesus.

Jesus was walking down a street in Jericho. Lots of people came to see Jesus, including a man named Zacchaeus. No one liked Zacchaeus very much because he was the chief tax collector. And he was quite wealthy because he stole money for himself. But Zacchaeus wanted to see Jesus. There was just one problem. He was too short to see over the crowd. So he ran ahead and climbed a sycamore-fig tree. When Jesus walked near the tree, he looked up and said to him, "Zacchaeus, come down immediately. I must stay at your house today." Do you think Zacchaeus was surprised?

1st Law of motion

Zacchaeus scrambled out of the tree and welcomed Jesus into his home for dinner. All the people saw this and began to complain, "He has gone to be the guest of a sinner." But Zacchaeus was so happy, he stood up and said to Jesus, "Look, LORD! Here and now I give half of my possessions to the poor, and if I have cheated anybody out of anything, I will pay back four times the amount." Jesus said to him, "Today salvation has come to this house, because this man, too, is a son of Abraham. For the Son of Man came to seek and to save the lost."

Zacchaeus' life was put in motion by his faith in Jesus. What changes did Zacchaeus make in the story?

Isaac Newton noticed how objects move. (Roll the ball to your child).
- Why did the ball move? (because it was pushed).
- Why did the ball stop? (because of the child's hand).
- So the ball was in motion until something stopped it. An object in motion stays in motion unless acted upon by an outside force; this is known as inertia.
- What was the outside force? (the hand).
- What if the ball is rolled, but no child touches it? (it will stop). Now roll the ball gently across the floor, so that it will stop by itself before it touches anything.
- Why does it stop? (bumps in the carpet, wind, friction, etc.). Outside forces keep the ball from rolling forever. The outside forces that work on any object in motion are friction and gravity.

FRICTION

Rub your hands together as hard and fast as you can. What do you feel? That is friction. It resists motion.

Can you think of any other examples of friction?

(shoes on a floor, bike brakes, stopping at the bottom of a slide, etc.)

What would the world be like if God had not created friction?

(Everything would be too slick to stand on. We would slip and slide everywhere).

GRAVITY

Gravity is the force that pulls all things toward the Earth. The ball is pulled against the floor by gravity, and stopped by the friction with the surface of the table/carpet. What would the world be like if God had not created gravity? (Everything would float such as food off your plate, water out of your cup).

What are some outside forces, besides friction and gravity? (Walls, water, people, etc).

1st Law of motion

Crazy Driver

1. Sit in the imaginary mini-van. Remember to buckle your imaginary seat belts. The teacher pretends to be a crazy driver.

2. Accelerate the mini-van. Everyone is pushed to the back of their seats. Your bodies are at rest; they want to remain at rest even though the van moved.

3. Stop the mini-van. Everyone is thrown forward. Your bodies are in motion; they want to remain in motion even though the van stopped.

4. Newton's First Law of motion states: *An object at rest will remain at rest, and an object in motion stays in motion, in the same direction, at the same speed, unless acted upon by an outside force.*

5. What happens if the mini-van is moving at a constant speed and the crazy driver turns left? Everyone is thrown to the right in the van. What happens if the crazy driver turns right? Everyone is thrown to the left in the van. The passengers' bodies want to remain traveling in the same direction, even though the van turned.

Pennies at Rest

1. Place the piece of paper half way off a table.

2. Place a penny on the paper, on the table side.

3. Form a hypothesis: What will happen if the paper is quickly pulled out?

4. Quickly jerk the paper in a downward motion.

5. Repeat the experiment with the pennies stacked higher.

6. The pennies stay in place because an object at rest will remain at rest. The speed at which you pull the paper overcomes the outside force of friction.

7. Form another hypothesis: What will happen if the paper is pulled out slowly?

8. Test the hypothesis by gently pulling on the paper. Why does the penny fall off the table?

New Covenant

Just as an outside force changes the motion of an object, Jesus Christ changes and transforms the lives of those who trust in Him. Look up the following Scriptures. Discuss how Jesus Christ changed the world, history, and the lives of people. What are some differences between the Old and New Testaments (or Old and New Covenants)?

- Exodus 19–24 and Luke 22:20
- Exodus 24:8 and Hebrews 8:6
- Exodus 24:3 and Galatians 6:2; 1 John 3:23–24; Romans 12:1
- Deuteronomy 12:11–14; 1 Kings 8:29–30, and 1 Corinthians 3:16
- Leviticus 1–7 and Hebrews 4:16

1st Law of motion

- As you go through your day, ask the children to point out moving objects, resting objects, and outside forces acting on objects. For instance:

  - Blood rushes to your head when an elevator stops ascending; blood rushes to your feet when an elevator stops descending.

  - Headrests are placed in cars to prevent injury in case of collision from the rear.

  - When a shampoo bottle is nearly empty, turn it upside down and shove it downward quickly. Then stop the bottle abruptly, the shampoo inside the bottle will continue its motion, and will thus be near the cap for easy removal.

  - What happens if you are riding a bike and the front wheel hits the curb? The bike stops. What happens to the rider?

- Look for evidence of the New Covenant in your church and in your personal faith.

- How can you let Jesus be a changing force in your life? How can you personally allow the will of God change your "direction and speed"?

- Do a character study to learn more about Isaac Newton. There are some good children's books available on him, but you can also use the short bios available at the end of this book. (See page 94)

- Consider the consequences to those who did NOT accept the change Jesus brought to the world. They remained believing "in the same direction, at the same speed" and denied the "outside force" that God sent to save the world.

Alien Headwear

Materials

Metal coat hanger, two tennis balls, duct tape.

1. Pull the coat hanger apart.
2. Use duct tape to attach the tennis balls to the opposite ends of the coat hanger.
3. Bend the coat hanger into the shape of a letter "M". Make a flat part to rest on top of your head. Make sure the ends of the hanger hang below the flat part (balancing point).
4. Carefully balance the hanger on your head. Then quickly spin in a circle. What do the tennis balls do? Why?

ACTIVITY

Study the difference in speed and acceleration:

- Speed is change in position per unit time, or distance/time. Velocity is also change in position per unit time, but includes the component of direction. For many purposes, the terms velocity and speed are interchangeable. Velocity is measured in an instant of time. It is a "snap shot" of a moving object.

- Acceleration is the rate of change of velocity, or velocity/time. It is measured over a period of time. If an object accelerates, its velocity is increased by the application of a force. Many sports announcers misuse the word "accelerate" to explain when a person is moving fast. But an object can be moving very fast and have no acceleration. If a runner is traveling at a constant velocity, he is not accelerating, no matter how fast he is going. If an object's velocity is not changing, then it is not accelerating. If an object is speeding up or slowing down then it has acceleration (positive acceleration for speeding up and negative acceleration for slowing down). So if the runner puts on a burst of speed for the finish line, then he has positive acceleration. If the runner gets tired and slows down, then he has negative acceleration.

NEWTON'S
SECOND LAW OF MOTION

Explore how God created objects to move. Define and explore the terms: mass, acceleration, and force. Memorize and understand that "Force = Mass x Acceleration", "F= MA" (even if the mathematical operator is not yet understood).

1. A beach ball or playground ball.
2. Latex exercise band without handles.
3. Playground slide.
4. Masking tape or painter's tape.
5. 3 or 4 toy cars of various sizes without any propulsion mechanism.

MATERIALS

BIG IDEA

MASS

God made lots of things that are small and lots of things that are large. What are some small, light weight things? (feather, paper, kitten, etc.) These have a small mass; they do not weigh much.

What are some big, heavy things? (car, house, tree, etc.) These have a large mass; they weigh a lot.

Mass is another way to say weight (as long as we are on Earth). In scientific terms, weight depends on the gravity acting on an object while mass never changes. An object floating in space has no weight, but the mass is the same as if it were on Earth.

ACCELERATION

God made lots of things that can move quickly from sitting still to moving very fast What are some things with high acceleration? (horse, race car, cheetah, rocket, humming bird, etc.)

God also made lots of things that slowly go from sitting still to moving. What are some things with low acceleration? (train, big truck, large eagle taking flight, etc.)

Acceleration is change in speed. For instance, a small car and a big truck are stopped at a red light. When the light turns green, they both begin to accelerate. Which one has the greatest acceleration? The small car will initially outrun the big truck. But out on the highway, the small car and the big truck may both be going the same speed.

FORCE

Hand the beach ball to a child. Ask him to press the ball between his hands with a lot of force (BIG squish). Now ask him to press the ball with a little force (tiny squish). Force is what causes the ball to change shape. Pass the ball to each child, allowing them to use force to change the shape of the ball.

Force is what causes an object to change movement, direction, or shape.

Can you apply a force to change the movement of the ball? Can you apply a force to change the direction of the ball?

Joel 2:11 says, "The LORD thunders at the head of His army; His forces are beyond number, and mighty is the army that obeys his command. The day of the LORD is great..."

This verse references the "day of the LORD" as the Great Tribulation. During the Great Tribulation, God's anger will be poured out on those who refused His plan of salvation through faith in Jesus Christ. God will direct His forces to change the movement, direction, and shape of this sinful world. Is there anything with more force than God? No.

Judgment must come because God is holy. He cannot be in the presence of sin. But God loves people so much, He sent His only Son Jesus to take the punishment for people. Those who accept the free gift of Jesus as their savior, those who walk in light and in truth, will not be held accountable for their sins. We will not experience the force of God's anger Those who reject the salvation through Jesus will be punished.

Romans 10:13 says, "Everyone who calls on the name of the LORD will be saved."

How can you "call on the name of the LORD"? (see Apply It section for guidance on salvation).

ACCELERATION WITHOUT MUCH MASS:

ACTIVITY 1

1. The teacher holds one end of the exercise band.
2. Ask a child to pull the other end of the band tight... tighter... tighter.
3. Form a hypothesis: *will the teacher be hurt when the child releases her end of the rubber band?*
4. Then ask the child to release the band.
5. Explain: the band has lots of acceleration; it speeds up quickly. But it has very little mass; it does not weigh much. It would hurt if it had mass. For instance, if there was a rock tied to the end of the rubber band would the teacher be hurt? (DO NOT TRY THIS; IT IS JUST A CONCEPT).

CAR DOWN A RAMP. SAME ACCELERATION, DIFFERENT MASS

ACTIVITY 2

1. Place a piece of masking tape across the end of the slide, similar to a finish line ribbon for the car to run through. Tape it tightly on both sides of the bottom of the slide.
2. Draw a starting line about 2 feet up the slide from the tape.
3. Choose the smallest car. Place the car at the starting line.
4. Form a hypothesis: Will the car break through the tape when released down the slide?
5. Test the hypothesis by releasing the car down the slide. Remind children not to push the car, but simply let go of the car.
   a. NOTE: if the smallest car does break through, double or triple the tape. Repeat the experiment and keep the tape the same for the remainder of the experiment.
6. Choose another car. Place it at the same starting line. Repeat steps 4 and 5 for all remaining cars.
   a. The larger cars will break through the tape because they have more mass, giving them more force.
   b. The smaller cars will not break through the tape because they have less mass, giving them less force.
7. Make sure the children understand that an increase in mass means an increase in force. Acceleration is constant since the car is pulled down the ramp by the acceleration of gravity. Cheer *"Force equals mass times acceleration!"* every time a car breaks through the tape.

Car down a ramp. Same mass, different acceleration

1. Place a piece of masking tape across the end of the slide, similar to a finish line ribbon for the car to run through. Tape it tightly on both sides of the bottom of the slide.

2. Choose one of the cars from activity 2 that did not break through the tape. Form a hypothesis: Will the car break through the tape when released down the slide?

3. Place the car at the starting line. Let it go. It should stop at the tape as before.

4. Place the same car at the same starting line. Form a hypothesis: Will the car break through the tape if it is PUSHED down the slide?

5. Instruct the student to give the car a fast push toward the tape. Test the hypothesis.

6. Allow students to take turns pushing the car with great acceleration so it breaks through the tape.

7. Make sure the children understand that an increase in acceleration means an increase in force. Mass is held constant since the same car is being used. Cheer *"Force equals mass times acceleration!"* every time a car breaks through the tape.

- Go bowling. Consider why bowlers use a heavy ball instead of a tennis ball?

- Study Romans 8:1 and 1 Thessalonians 5:9. Is this good news for believers?

- When God first created the world, everything was perfect. But one day, Adam and Eve disobeyed God, and the world became imperfect. Through the generations, people have done the same. At one time or another, every person chooses to do wrong things. We hurt other people, we are selfish, and we often forget about God. We all have sin in our hearts. Sin separates us from God. But God does not stop loving us, even when we sin. He loves us so much, He sent Jesus. Jesus took the punishment for everything we have done wrong. Because of this amazing act of love, all the sin you have ever committed can be forgiven. Jesus is waiting for you to ask. When you believe Jesus died for you and ask for forgiveness, Jesus wipes away all of your sins. God is so pleased with this, you become His child. When you are a part of God's family, you can talk to him freely. And you can know that you will live with God forever in heaven.

  - Talk to your child about admitting that he has sinned and needs forgiveness.

  - Trusting in Jesus is the only way to be saved from the punishment of sin.

  - Pray for your child, asking God to convict his heart and bring him to faith in Christ. Ask for wisdom to lead your child to Jesus.

  - Helpful verses: 1 John 1:9, John 1:12,

- "The bigger they are, the harder they fall" is a common phrase. It is true that an object with more mass will hit the ground with more force, but it will not hit the ground with more acceleration. No matter what the mass, all objects fall with the same acceleration.

2ND LAW OF MOTION

GO BEYOND

ACCELERATION OF GRAVITY
(this activity requires 3 people):

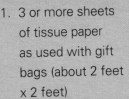

MATERIALS

1. 3 or more sheets of tissue paper as used with gift bags (about 2 feet x 2 feet)

2. 5 or more objects of different masses that you can safely drop from about 6 feet (plastic bottle, marble, a penny, shoe, feather, etc.)

1. Ask your students to line up the 5 objects to be dropped in order of mass, smallest to largest. They can estimate the comparative mass.

2. One child (or adult) stands on a chair with the object of smallest mass held high, while two children hold a piece of the tissue paper by its 4 corners stretched taut between them directly under the object of smallest mass.

3. Form a hypothesis: Will the object with the least mass tear through the tissue paper when it is dropped by the person on the chair?

4. Test the hypothesis. Did it hit with high force and tear the paper? Or low force and bounce?

5. Remind the children that gravity works the same on all objects, so the acceleration of each object is 9.8 m/s2. Therefore, their different masses will give them different forces.

6. Repeat steps 2-5 with the remaining objects in ascending order of mass. You should see an increase in force as the paper begins to tear. Reuse the paper if it withstands the test; replace it if the object tears through or corners tear away.

7. Make sure the children understand that an increase in mass means an increase in force. The acceleration of gravity is constant.

IF YOUR CHILD CAN MULTIPLY OR USE A CALCULATOR

Force = Mass x Acceleration. Where Force is in Newtons (kg.m/s2), mass is in kilograms, and acceleration is in m/s2.

1. How much force is required to accelerate a 2 kg mass at 3 m/s2?

   Solution: Force = 2 x 3

   Answer: Force = 6 Newtons

2. How much force is required to accelerate a 50 kg mass at 2 m/s2?

   Solution: Force = 50 x 2

   Answer: Force = 100 Newtons

2ND LAW OF MOTION

Newton's
Third Law of Motion

Understand Newton's Third Law of Motion. Demonstrate that for every action there is an equal and opposite reaction. Explore the variables associated with Newton's Third Law of Motion.

MATERIALS

1. Two rulers or paint sticks.
2. 10 pennies.
3. Tape.
4. Empty soda can with tab intact.
5. Medium size nail.
6. Kite string or thread.
7. Empty balloons.
8. Drinking straws.

BIG IDEA

Ask the children to sit down in chairs. What are you sitting on? When you sit in the chair does your body push down on it? (Ask the children to pick up your chair with you in it, then try again without you in it). The force of gravity pushes your body down into your chair. But there is another force working too; it works opposite to the force you are putting down on your chair. What do you think it might be? The chair is pushing back up on your body! If the chair did not push you up, what would happen? (You would fall down).

These two forces are action and reaction forces. Isaac Newton noticed that forces come in pairs. His third law states that **For every action there is an equal and opposite reaction.** Say that several times together.

What this means is that when two forces contact each other; the size of one force equals the size of the other. It also means that the direction of one force is opposite to the direction of the other force. Think about a duck swimming in a pond: The duck uses its webbed feet to push the water backwards, therefore the water pushes the duck forward. This action and reaction force makes it possible for the duck to swim.

Consider:
- a bird flying: the bird's wings push the air backwards, therefore the air pushes the bird forward.
- a car driving: the car's tires push the asphalt backwards, therefore the asphalt pushes the car forward.
- a horse galloping: the horse's hooves push the ground backwards, therefore the ground pushes the horse forward.

3RD LAW OF MOTION

BIG IDEA CONTINUED...

Our lives can be like Newton's Third Law of Motion. Every time we add something positive to our lives (action), less negative things (opposite reaction) are in our lives. The more good habits you have, the less bad habits you have. For instance, the more you serve others, the less selfish you will be.

Philippians 2:3 tells us, "Do nothing out of selfish ambition or vain conceit. Rather, in humility value others above yourselves."

In addition to serving, what are some other positives God wants us to have? Love, peace, joy, kindness, grace, etc. What are the negatives God wants us to leave behind? Hate, anger, meanness, impatience, discontent, etc.

ACTIVITY 1

ACTIVITIES

SHARING SUCCESS

1. Philippians 2:3 tells us, "Do nothing out of selfish ambition or vain conceit. Rather, in humility value others above yourselves."

2. Pair the children. Ask them to tell one story of success with their partner. A story of success could be something they feel proud of, an achievement, winning in sports, doing well on a test, having a good attitude, finishing a challenging project, etc.

3. Remind the children to listen carefully to their partners' story. Give a time limit for each child to share his/her story.

4. Then ask each child to share his/her partner's success story with the group. Sharing someone else's success is one way to value others above yourself. Encourage the positive aspects of the success stories.

ACTIVITY 2

BALLOON LAUNCH

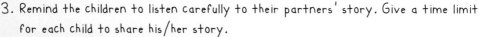

1. Give each student a balloon.

2. Ask them to stand still, but get the balloons to the other side of the room.

3. Now place a length of kite string through a straw. Tie or hold the ends of the string on the opposite sides of the room.

4. Blow up the balloon, but do not tie it. Tape the balloon to the straw.

5. Release the balloon so it races across the room.

6. Allow students to design races and experiment with string angle and balloon volume.

7. For every action there is an equal and opposite reaction. The action is the balloon pushing air out; the reaction is the air inside the balloon pushing it forward.

3RD LAW OF MOTION

ACTIVITY 3

PENNY BUMP

1. Line up the two rulers side by side on the table about one inch apart.
2. Line up five of the pennies between the rulers. Place them so they are all touching, about one inch from the end of the rulers.
3. Tape the ends of the rulers to the table so they are stable.
4. Place the sixth penny at one end, between the rulers.
5. Form a hypothesis: What will happen to the five pennies if the sixth penny is flicked at the five pennies?
6. Test the hypothesis:
7. When you flick the coin it bumps into the first coin; this is the "action." The coin tries to move but bumps into the next coin; this is the "reaction." And that coin bumps into the next and the next; another and another "reaction." The force is passed from coin to coin until it is passed to the last coin in the line. There is nothing holding the last coin, so it flies off while the other four remain steady.
8. Repeat steps 4–6 flicking two coins and three coins. Repeat the phrase, "for every action there is an equal and opposite reaction" every time the coins fly off.

3RD LAW OF MOTION

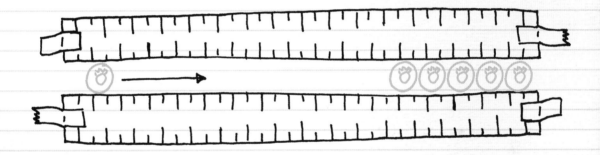

SODA CAN

1. Lay the soda can on its side. Use the nail to punch 2 holes across from each other on the bottom edge of the empty soda can. Before removing the nail, push the nail to one side in order to bend the metal and make a slanted hole; make sure all holes slant the same direction.
2. Bend the tab straight up, fill the can with water, and suspend the can by a string.
3. What happens?
4. For every action there is an equal and opposite reaction. The action is the water pouring out of the can; the reaction is the can spinning.
5. Allow students to experiment with four holes or larger holes. How can you get the can to spin the other direction? What if two holes point one way and two holes point the other way?

ACTIVITY 4

- Look for examples of Newton's Third Law of Motion out in the world. Examples may include: rotary lawn sprinkler, a ball bouncing, a dog running, a cat sleeping on a chair, etc.

- Apply Newton's 3rd Law of Motion to life:
  - Make two lists: positive habits and negative habits.
  - Find one bad habit that would be easy to stop. Work to change that bad habit.
  - As soon as you change it, do you notice a new positive habit in your life? Modify your list accordingly.
  - Find another bad habit to change. And so forth. Soon you will have so many good habits, you will not have time for the bad habits.

- Foot washing. Read John 13:5-17. How did Jesus serve his disciples? Wash the children's feet, have them wash each other's feet, ask them to wash your feet.

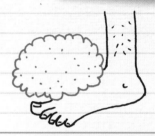

GO BEYOND

- Study Isaiah 40: 26-31. What examples of Newton's Third Law of Motion are mentioned?

- Study the fruit of the spirit in Galatians 5:22-23. Praise these behaviors as you notice them. Encourage children to replace negative habits with positive habits.

- Allow students to design and perform other coin experiments using other sizes of coin.

- Study the inventions of Hero of Alexandria in the first century B.C., especially his "aeolipile." How is it similar to the soda can from Activity 3? (See page 25)

- Ask students to demonstrate Newton's Third Law of Motion using a pool table and billiard balls or marbles on a smooth surface.

3RD LAW OF MOTION

COEFFICIENT OF FRICTION

Explore friction on an inclined plane.

Determine the relative coefficient of friction of various materials.

MATERIALS

1. A current newspaper.
2. One pencil for each child.
3. One piece of paper for each child.
4. Baby oil or vegetable oil.
5. Gentle incline plane such as a playground slide (alternatively a collapsed folding table, ironing board without a pad, or broad smooth board will suffice).
6. Five to ten small, non-rolling objects of similar size made from various materials (block of wood, rubber soled shoe, leather soled shoe, plastic cup, stuffed animal, metal pan, small article of clothing, small article of wet clothing, rock, piece of broken concrete, pine cone, etc.).
7. Wax paper.

Before the activity, find one object that slides rather slowly. Get two of those items that are identical, such as a pair of rubber soled shoes.

Also, before the activity, use tape or marker to make a "starting line" for sliding objects down the slide. It needs to be a few inches below the top of the incline.

BIG IDEA

Have you ever had trouble? Seen trouble? Been in trouble? Trouble is everywhere in this world. Study the newspaper together, finding all of the trouble and bad news. This world can be a pretty scary place, but there is great news.

John 16:33 Jesus says, "I have told you these things, so that in me you may have peace. In this world you will have trouble. *But take heart! I have overcome the world.*"

What do you think "take heart" means? Be brave, don't run away, conquer, and overcome obstacles. That would probably be impossible, but we are not alone. Jesus is with us. He has overcome the world. He chose to die on the cross. He overcame death. He can overcome ANYTHING!

What are some troubles or obstacles that you have overcome? How did Jesus help you?

Jesus' love never stops overcoming, just like gravity never stops pulling. In this lesson we are going to learn about how gravity overcomes the force of friction.

FRICTION

Some objects are very slippery. Can you think of slippery things? (ice, soap, wet tile, wet bathtub, etc.). Some objects are rough or less slippery. Can you think of things that are less slippery? (shoes, wood, grass, etc.)

The word for why some things do not slip is friction. Say "friction" several times. Friction is the force that tries to stop motion.

- Have you ever skinned your knee? Friction between your knee and the ground caused your skin to be hurt.
- Have you ever slipped on a wet floor? Not enough friction between your feet and the floor caused you to fall.
- Have you ever heard your sneakers squeak on linoleum? That is the sound of the friction created as the rubber on your shoes slides across the floor.
- Have you ever heard tires squeal on pavement? That is the sound of the friction created as the rubber tires slide across the road.

The coefficient of friction is determined by the materials touching each other. For example, metal ice skate blades on ice have a low coefficient of friction (like your feet on the wet floor). Rubber car tires on pavement have a high coefficient of friction (like your knee on the ground).

Are you thankful that God gave us friction? What would our world be like without friction? (No one could stand up because their feet would always be slipping, everything would slide off the table, lots of car wrecks, etc.)

SLICK PENCIL

ACTIVITY 1

This can be messy. It's best if done outside with wipes ready. Consider using smocks/aprons as oil can stain clothing.

1. Give each child a pencil and paper.

2. Ask them to write their first names very small and neatly. Can you feel the friction between your fingers and the pencil?

3. Take their pencils. Let the children watch as you use your fingers or a tissue to coat the shaft of each pencil in oil.

4. Give the pencils back to the children. Ask them to write their names again very small and neatly. Remind them not to wipe their hands on their clothes. Was there more or less friction between your fingers and the oily pencil?

Clean up: wipes or washing with soap will clean hands. Warm water and dish soap can be used to clean the pencils.

WILL IT SLIDE?

ACTIVITY 2

1. Make two signs to create categories in which to place objects after they are tested down the slide: "High coefficient of friction" and "Low coefficient of friction."

2. Ask the child to climb to the top of the slide/incline plane. If there are many children, have them safely take turns throughout the activity.

3. Give the child one object to place at the top of the incline/starting line.

4. Form a hypothesis: Will it slide?

5. Test the hypothesis. Ask the child to release the object, without pushing it. Was the hypothesis correct? Did it have a high or low coefficient of friction?

6. Place the object in the correct category.

7. Repeat steps 1–6 until all of the objects have been tested.

WILL IT SLIDE FASTER?

1. Gather the pair of identical objects determined before the activity.
2. Tape a piece of wax paper around the bottom of one of the objects.
3. Hold the pair of objects side by side at the top of the incline/starting line.
4. Form a hypothesis: Which one will slide faster?
5. Test the hypothesis. Release both objects simultaneously without pushing. What happened? Did one of the objects experience less friction?
6. Place the objects in the correct categories.
7. See "Go Beyond" section.

APPLY IT

- Look around for examples of objects with a low coefficient of friction, things that are slippery. Look around for examples of objects with a high coefficient of friction, things that are less slippery.

- Search for squeaky hinges, swings, and toys; their coefficient of friction is too high. Use a can of lubricant oil to lower the coefficient of friction and stop them from squeaking.

- Any time you notice an example of friction, repeat the memory verse. John 16:33 Jesus says, "I have told you these things, so that in me you may have peace. In this world you will have trouble. But take heart! I have overcome the world."

GO BEYOND

- Let the children explore other ways to change the coefficient of friction between the objects and the slide: water, oil/cooking spray, dust, felt or fabric, rubber, etc.

- 1 Timothy 6:3-10 discusses friction between people (verse 5). What do you think Paul means?

- Study how some scientific discoveries serve as building blocks for further discoveries. Use the biography section at the end of the book in your studies. (See page 91).

Regarding friction, tradition has it that the basic rules of sliding friction were discovered by Leonardo da Vinci (1452–1519) but were never published. In 1699, Guillaume Amontons rediscovered and furthered da Vinci's work. Then in 1785 Charles - Augustin de Coulomb studied the influence of the four most important factors on friction: the makeup of the materials' surface, the size of the surface area, the pressure on the surfaces, and the length of time that the surfaces are in contact.

(reference: Dowson, Duncan (1997). *History of Tribology, 2nd Edition*. Professional Engineering Publishing. ISBN 1-86058-070-X)

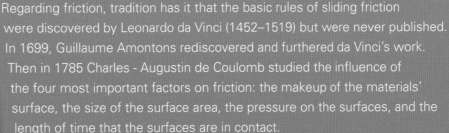

FRICTION

STATIC ELECTRICITY

To understand static electricity. Define and identify insulators (resistors), conductors, and capacitors.

MATERIALS

1. One inflated balloon for each student (preferably not helium inflated).

2. A mirror.

3. A plastic playground slide.

4. Optional: wooly sweater or fleece.

Do you enjoy taking shortcuts? They might save you some time. They can be fun and exciting. Can shortcuts also get you into trouble? Have you ever taken a shortcut that turned out badly?

When God told Moses to build the Ark of the Covenant, Moses did not take any shortcuts. He followed God's instructions exactly. God told Moses how to build the Ark (Exodus 37:1-9), how to carry the Ark on two wooden poles (Exodus 37:4-5), and that no one should touch the Ark (Numbers 4:15).

BIG IDEA

Later on, King David was in charge of the Ark of the Covenant's care. He thought of a shortcut. He decided it would be a good idea to put the Ark on a cart pulled by oxen instead of carrying it on two poles as God had instructed. Do you think that this sounds easier? Read the following Bible passage from 2 Samuel 6: 1-8 to discover how David's shortcut turned out.

THE ARK BROUGHT TO JERUSALEM

David again brought together all the able young men of Israel—thirty thousand. He and all his men went to Baalah in Judah to bring up from there the Ark of God, which is called by the name of the Lord Almighty, who is enthroned between the cherubim on the Ark. They set the Ark of God on a new cart and brought it from the house of Abinadab, which was on the hill. Uzzah and Ahio, sons of Abinadab, were guiding the new cart with the Ark of God on it, and Ahio was walking in front of it. David and all Israel were celebrating with all their might before the Lord, with castanets, harps, lyres, timbrels, sistrums and cymbals.

When they came to the threshing floor of Nakon, Uzzah reached out and took hold of the Ark of God, because the oxen stumbled. The Lord's anger burned against Uzzah because of his irreverent act; therefore God struck him down, and he died there beside the Ark of God.

Then David was angry because the Lord's wrath had broken out against Uzzah, and to this day that place is called Perez Uzzah.

God gives us commands for His perfect reasons. David took a shortcut that disobeyed what God told him to do, and it did not turn out well. We do not always understand God's reasons; but we do not have to understand them to trust and obey. After today's lesson, you may have an idea about one reason God told the people not to touch the Ark of the Covenant.

Isaiah 40:28 ... [God's] understanding no one can fathom.

STATIC ELECTRICITY

Have you ever felt an electrical shock? Like when you walk across the carpet, then touch a door knob? You were filled with static electricity!!! God made many forms of electricity all around us. Can you think of any other places you see electricity? (lightning, a fuzzy blanket crackling in the dark, your brain conducting messages, getting shocked while petting a fuzzy cat, manmade electricity for light bulbs, etc).

Sometimes when two objects rub together, one object is an insulator, or resistor (that means it does not carry electricity easily) and the other object is a conductor (that means it does carry electricity easily). When a conductor and a resistor/insulator rub together, electrons jump from one object to the other to produce static electricity.

You can feel, hear, and sometimes even see when the electricity discharges. This is a shock! The electricity is always trying to find the ground, and it will flow through the conductor to get to the ground.

Charged Balloon

ACTIVITY 1

1. Ask, "How can you make a balloon stick to a wall?" Before the balloons have been handled too much, allow the children to try to make them stick to the wall.

2. Rub the balloon on your hair or sweater. Have the children look at their hair in the mirror as it sticks to the balloon. The balloon picks up a charge of static electricity from your hair. Now the balloon is a capacitor; a capacitor is anything that holds a charge.

3. Form a hypothesis: Will the balloon stick to the wall now that it has an electrical charge?

4. Test the hypothesis: try to stick it to the wall again. The balloon will stick until its charge is transferred into the wall.

WIGGLE, SLIDE, & SHOCK

ACTIVITY 2

A dry, windy day and plastic playground slides are essential. Nylon or wool clothing is preferable.

1. Make 3 paper signs. Two as necklaces for the children, "Conductor" and "Capacitor." And one for the slide "Insulator/resistor." An insulator does not allow an electrical charge to flow freely.

2. Ask a child with medium length, straight, dry hair to sit at the top of the slide and wiggle, wiggle, wiggle against the plastic. Hang the "Capacitor" sign around his/her neck. Make sure he/she does not touch any metal that

goes to ground or he/she will lose his/her charge.

3. While he/she is wiggling, explain: The child is storing static electricity; he/she is a capacitor. Static electricity from the plastic slide causes the child's hair to stand up. The child's motion takes electrons away from the child, leaving him/her with a positive charge. These positive charges repel each other along each strand of hair, making the hairs stand apart.

4. Ask the child to slide down, but keep his/her feet OFF the ground, then have the "Capacitor" child reach out and touch the finger of another child who is wearing the "Conductor" sign. Explain that the electricity wants to reach the ground, so it will jump from the capacitor child on the insulating slide to the conductor child standing with his/her feet on the ground. A conductor allows an electrical charge to move easily from atom to atom.

5. Can you see the shock? Can you hear the shock? Can you feel the shock?

6. Have the students take turns being the capacitor and the conductor.

7. Note: if the shocks are not sufficient, put a wooly sweater or fleece on the "capacitor" child.

APPLY IT

- Every time you or your child experiences a shock, say **"STATIC ELECTRICITY!"** Repeat the memory verse Isaiah 40:28 …

> [God's] understanding no one can fathom.

- From a safe distance, watch a lightning storm together. Explain how the clouds act as capacitors, storing static electricity created by friction of ice crystals within the clouds. When the charge becomes high enough, the electricity will jump to the ground like a great big shock.

  - On a side note: The heat from the lightning makes the air rapidly expand creating a sonic boom. This is the sound of thunder. Even though the flash of lightning and crash of thunder occur at the same moment, you usually do not experience them at the same time. This is due to the difference in the slower speed of sound as compared to the faster speed of light. The thunder from a bolt of lightning that is 1 mile away will take about 5 seconds to reach you. The thunder from a bolt of lightning that is 2 miles away will take about 10 seconds to reach you. The thunder from a bolt of lightning that is 3 miles away will take about 15 seconds to reach you. Etc.

- We know the danger of electricity. We often see warning signs to tell us not to go near electric pylons and towers. but electricity can be used to good effect with light and

STATIC ELECTRICITY

- Ask the children, could the Ark of the Covenant have acted as a capacitor?

  Yes. It could have stored electricity as the dry desert air blew over it.

Study scientist Benjamin Franklin (1706-1790) flying a kite in a thunderstorm.
[Warning: do not attempt!]

- In a low humidity environment, tear (do not cut) a piece of paper into confetti size pieces and scatter them around the table. Give each child a hard plastic comb. Allow them to comb their hair, then experiment with holding the comb over the paper without touching the paper. What happens? Why do you think this happens? Perform the "Opposites attract" activity to draw conclusions about the cause of the observation.

power. As you go through the day, point out any good uses of electricity and any danger signs for electricity. Now there is something that is even more dangerous than electricity– and there is no good in it whatsoever. Sin. Sin if unforgiven separates us from the love of God forever. All sin deserves God's anger and punishment. Uzzah should have remembered God's instructions not to touch the Ark of the covenant. Uzzah died as a result of his action. If we do not trust in Jesus Christ to save us from our sins we will face eternal death.

OPPOSITES ATTRACT:

ACTIVITY

1. Two inflated balloons with a string tied to each balloon,
2. Empty aluminum can,
3. Wooly fabric.

1. Rub the two balloons on strings one at a time on the wooly fabric.

2. Move the balloons together. Do they attract or repel each other? Explain that rubbing the balloons on the wooly fabric creates static electricity, making both balloons negatively charged and leaving the fabric positively charged. Since both balloons are negatively charged, they repel each other.

   Alike charges repel, opposite charges attract.

3. Rub one of the balloons back and forth on your hair then slowly it pull it away. Ask someone nearby what they can see or if there's nobody else around try looking in a mirror. Explain that rubbing the balloon on your hair creates static electricity. The balloon has a negative charge while your hair has a positive charge. Since opposite charges attract, your hair rises up to meet the balloon.

4. Place the empty aluminum can on its side on a smooth table. Rub the balloon on your hair again hold the balloon close to the can. As the can rolls towards the balloon, slowly move the balloon away to make the can follow. The negatively charged balloon actually creates a positively charged area around the can, which causes it to be attracted.

5. What happens if the can touches the balloon?

ACIDS AND BASES

Explore how acids taste sour and bases taste bitter.
Feel the rough texture of acid and the slick texture of base.

MATERIALS

1. A serving of delicious cooked green scrambled eggs (add a few drops of green food coloring while scrambling).

2. The book *Green Eggs and Ham* by Dr. Seuss (optional).

3. Three to five sour foods or drinks (such as orange juice, lemon, sour candy, green grapes, sour cream, pickles, tomatoes, etc.).

4. Three to five bitter foods (Brussels sprouts, unsweetened cocoa, baking soda, orange peel, coffee, persimmon, etc.).

5. A spoon or fork for each child.

6. Liquid soap.

7. Vinegar.

   [Note: do not use any sweet foods.]

What tastes good?

How do you know it tastes good?

You have to try a food before you know if it is yummy or yucky.

What have you discovered that is good about **God** and **God's** creation?

BIG IDEA

He is perfect, He is good to people, He created Earth, He is love, He gives us good things, He keeps His promises, He sent His perfect son, He is the good shepherd, etc.

We experience the LORD's goodness and learn to trust in him. We are nourished by His grace and love.

If you fill your body with bad food, what happens? You get sick and weak. What do you think will happen to your soul if you fill it with bad influences from this world? Your soul will be sick.

> **Psalm 34:8 "O taste and see that the LORD is good: blessed is the man that trusts in Him."**

God created different foods to taste different to our tongues.

What is your favorite food?

What is your least favorite food?

Our tongues can EVEN taste the chemistry of a food. Today we are going to determine if a food is an acidic food or a basic food. Acids taste sour and bases taste bitter.

ACIDS AND BASES

YUCKY?

1. Without letting the children taste the eggs, ask if they think the scrambled eggs will taste delicious.

2. Read the following poem.

3. Ask, "Do you think these things would taste good? Do you want to try these foods?"

   a. Alternatively, read Green Eggs and Ham by Dr. Seuss. Ask, "Why do you think Sam wanted to share his green eggs and ham with the man? Why didn't the man want to try them?"

I WOULD LIKE TO SHARE

For breakfast, I will share my pudding,
With tuna fish mixed up in it.

For lunch, some tasty ice cream?
With pickles sliced upon it?

For dinner, would you like scrambled eggs?
Green and cooked up thick?

And now, oh dear, oh pardon me!
I think I may be sick!

4. Have the children try the green eggs. Ask them how they taste.

5. Psalm 34:8 says, "O taste and see that the **LORD** is good: blessed is the man that trusts in him."

   a. "Taste and see" suggests, "Try it. You will like it!" Would you have known the eggs were good if you hadn't tasted them? What are some things you have tried to determine if God is good?

   b. When you first learned about Jesus, were you scared to be his friend? A lot of people are afraid to trust Jesus. Do you like being friends with Jesus?

   c. Do you want to share what you know about Jesus with others? It is important for us to be like Sam I Am; we need to take the good news of Jesus to our friends. And be kind and persistent showing them His love.

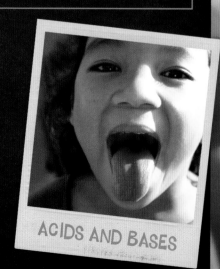

ACIDS AND BASES

Acid / Base Taste Test

ACTIVITY 2

1. Have children make two signs "SOUR ACIDS" and "BITTER BASES" to create categories to place foods in after they are tasted.

2. Choose one of the foods. Form a hypothesis: is it sour or bitter?

3. Have everyone taste the food, using spoons or forks if needed. Determine if it is sour or bitter. In general, bitter foods do not taste good to children, while acids do. Place the food in the correct category. (Note: it may be a good idea to have a drink of water between tastes.)

4. Repeat steps 2 and 3 for the remaining foods and drinks. With every conclusion, mention the phrase, "acids are sour and bases are bitter"

Acid / Base Feel Test

ACTIVITY 3

1. Have the children feel a drop of vinegar between their fingers. It feels slightly rough.

2. Ask them to lick the vinegar. It is a sour acid. Acids feel rough.

3. Feel a drop of lemon juice. Does it feel rough?

4. Ask the children to feel a drop of liquid soap between their fingers. It is slick.

5. DO NOT LICK the SOAP. Bases feel slick.

6. Now go wash hands.

7. Mix a little baking soda with a water to make a paste. Does it feel slick?

- The next meal or snack time, ask the children to hypothesize whether foods are acids or bases. Use this opportunity to review the memory verse from Psalm 34:8:

APPLY IT

> "O taste and see that the **LORD** is good: blessed is the **man** that trusts in him."

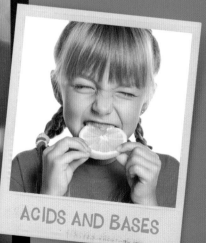

ACIDS AND BASES

- Find other acids and bases.

  - o Bases: most cleaning solutions are basic and slick to the touch, like window cleaner and laundry detergent. Coffee is bitter and basic.

  - o Acids: fizzy sodas contain carbonic acid and phosphoric acid.

- Study the Great Commission in Matthew 28:16-20. Discuss with your students real strategies for telling others about Christ.

Study Svante Arrhenius. (See page 91) His simple definition of acids and bases is one of the oldest, but is still widely used.

Arrhenius described acids as hydrogen ion (H+) donors and bases as hydroxide ion (OH-) donors when mixed with water.

RED CABBAGE INDICATOR

ACTIVITIES

MATERIALS

1. One red cabbage.
2. Knife.
3. Boiling water.
4. Coffee filters (optional).
5. Two large glass jars.
6. Eight smaller glass containers.
7. Household chemicals: *ammonia, baking soda, washing soda, lemon juice, vinegar, cream of tartar, several crushed antacid pills, seltzer water.*

[NOTE: Wear goggles for this experiment. Only adults should handle household chemicals, especially ammonia and vinegar.]

Red cabbage contains flavin. This is a pigment that will turn red in acid, purple in neutral solutions, and yellow/green in base.

1. Chop cabbage until you have at least two cups. Place the chopped cabbage in the large glass jar and pour boiling water over the cabbage. Let it sit for at least ten minutes.

2. Pour the liquid into the other large glass jar, leaving the chopped cabbage behind. This blue/purple liquid has an approximately neutral pH of 7. This is the acid/base indicator.

3. Pour about 2 tablespoons of the indicator into each of the smaller glass jars.

4. Add various household chemicals to the indicator until a color change is observed. WARNING: use separate jars for each chemical. Do not mix household chemicals.

5. The pH scale is a measure of how acidic or basic something is.

   • pH 0 to 7 are acids. Strong acids have a lower pH. For instance, battery acid has a pH of about 1.
   • pH 7 is neutral, like distilled water.
   • pH 7 to 14 are bases. Strong bases have a higher pH. For instance, bleach has a pH of about 13.

	ACID	ACID	ACID	NEUTRAL	BASE	BASE	BASE
pH	2	4	6	7	8	10	12
colour	Red	Purple	Violet	Blue/Purple	Blue	Blue/Green	Green/Yellow

6. Have older children create a data table to record the results. For example:

Household chemical	Color	Acid? Base? Or Neutral?

7. Allow children to perform a neutralization experiment by first adding vinegar to the indicator until a red color is obtained, then adding baking soda until the color returns to neutral red/purple. Warning: perform this experiment outside or over a bucket as excessive fizzing occurs.

8. pH paper can be made using coffee filters. Simply soak the filters in the red cabbage juice solution for several hours. Hang it up to dry, then cut it into strips. These strips can be used in the future to test the pH of solutions.

9. All chemicals used in this experiment may be washed down the drain with running water. Throw the chopped cabbage pulp away soon because it becomes rancid.

Combustion Reactions: How a Fire Burns

Understand combustion reactions. Experiment with what a candle needs to burn.

MATERIALS

1. A small tea candle.
2. Lighter.
3. Vinegar.
4. Baking soda.
5. Baking yeast.
6. Hydrogen peroxide.
7. A small plastic or paper cup.
8. A large inverted clear glass jar under which both the candle and the small cup can sit.
9. Watch with a second hand.
10. Two labels: "CO_2" and "O_2".

[Hazard: do not use a tall candle.]

HOW A FIRE BURNS

Would you like to hear an amazing story of three real heroes?

BIG IDEA

This story is from the Bible. From Daniel 3: There was once a great kingdom called the Babylonian Empire. This story begins with the ruler of this empire, King Nebuchadnezzar. He was a very powerful man with lots of money. Nearly everyone thought he was the greatest king ever. King Nebuchadnezzar agreed that maybe he was the greatest king ever. He was so very pleased with his rule that he built a great big golden statue of himself. He wanted to show off his new statue, so he threw a huge party and invited all of the important people from the kingdom. Three of the young men who came to the party worshiped the One True God. Their names were Shadrach, Meshach and Abednego. They were probably laughing and having a good time until the herald loudly proclaimed, "Nations and peoples of every language, this is what you are commanded to do: As soon as you hear the sound of the horn, flute, zither, lyre, harp, pipe and all kinds of music, you must fall down and worship the image of gold that King Nebuchadnezzar has set up. Whoever does not fall down and worship will immediately be thrown into a blazing furnace." Daniel 3:4-7

Shadrach, Meshach and Abednego had a big problem with worshiping a golden statue of Nebuchadnezzar. They knew God's perfect law and did not want to break it. Exodus 20:4-5 says, "You shall not make for yourself an image in the form of anything in heaven above or on the earth beneath or in the waters below. You shall not bow down to them or worship them."

So the three young men had to make a decision, obey God or obey the king. Shadrach, Meshach and Abednego knew that they were supposed to obey their earthly leaders, but they were not to obey their leaders if their commands broke God's perfect law, even if it meant they would be killed for their faith. What would you have done? It would have been very easy for them to bow down just like everyone else. But when the music stopped, these three stood tall. King Nebuchadnezzar was enraged. He thought he was greater than God. Shadrach, Meshach, and Abednego were brought before the furious king. Imagine how they felt standing in front of all of those people. They could probably feel the heat and smell the smoke from the fiery furnace, but they did not back down. They turned to the angry king and said, "If we are thrown into the blazing furnace, the God we serve is able to deliver us from it, and he will deliver us from Your Majesty's hand. But even if he does not, we want you to know, Your Majesty, that we will not serve your gods or worship the image of gold you have set up."

So King Nebuchadnezzar followed through on his threat. He had them tied up, heated the furnace extra hot, and then threw Shadrach, Meshach, and Abednego into it. The king peered into the furnace to make sure they were burning, but what he saw surprised him. The young men were not burning. They were walking around. Their ropes were gone, but the thing that really shocked Nebuchadnezzar was the fact that he saw four men in the fire. He said, "Didn't we throw three men into the fire? I see four men walking around in there and one of the men looks like the son of the gods." Who do you think the fourth man was?

The King had the men brought out of the furnace. They were not burned. They did not even smell like smoke. Only the ropes that bound them were burned away by the fire. Nebuchadnezzar was so impressed that he worshiped the One True God, promoted Shadrach, Meshach, and Abednego, and made a law that no one could say anything bad about the One True God. God had protected them and used their unflinching faith to sway the mind of a king!

These three young men were very brave for God. Have you ever been brave for God? Can you think of a time when you might have to stand up for what you believe, even when no one around you does? Remember this amazing story of Shadrach, Meshach, and Abednego, and be brave for God.

Deuteronomy 31:6 tells us to "Be strong and courageous ... for the LORD your God goes with you."

Today we are going to learn more about fire. We will better understand the great miracle God performed when he protected Shadrach, Meshach, and Abednego from burning. Have you ever seen something burn? (sticks, fire place, grill, candle, forest, cigarette, etc.)

God created fire as a really special tool for people to use. What are some reasons people use fire? (keep warm, cook food, clear debris, fireworks, car engines, etc.)

Fire burning is a combustion reaction. Say "combustion reaction" several times. Combustion reactions are very exciting, and almost all of them follow these rules:

- Combustion reactions need a carbon fuel source, like wood, paper, or gasoline.

- Combustion reactions need oxygen gas (O_2). Just like people and animals need oxygen to breathe, fire needs oxygen to burn. The air is about 21% oxygen.

- Combustion reactions make heat and/or light.

- Combustion reactions make carbon dioxide gas (CO_2). Just like people and animals breathe out carbon dioxide gas, fire produces carbon dioxide gas. The air is about 0.04% carbon dioxide. Note, this is different than carbon monoxide gas (CO), which is toxic in moderate concentrations.

- Combustion reactions make water vapor.

- As written in a rudimentary chemical reaction:

$$\text{Fuel} + O_2 \text{ (gas)} \rightarrow \text{heat} + CO_2 \text{ (gas)} + H_2O \text{ (gas)}$$

- Note: our atmosphere is about 78% nitrogen gas, which is largely inert.

CANDLE UNDER A JAR

ACTIVITIES

CANDLE UNDER A JAR:

1. Light the candle and let it burn for a few minutes.
2. Form a hypothesis: what will happen to the flame if the jar is placed over the candle?
3. Test the hypothesis. Why do you think the flame goes out? (not enough oxygen)
4. Re-light the candle. Clear the carbon dioxide out of the jar by blowing into it several times or rinsing it with water.
5. Form a hypothesis: how many seconds will it take for the flame to go out when the jar is placed over the candle?
6. Test the hypothesis and write the number of seconds down.

CANDLE PLUS CARBON DIOXIDE (CO₂) UNDER A JAR:

1. Light the candle.
2. Form a hypothesis: will the flame burn longer or shorter if carbon dioxide is added to the jar?
3. Place the "CO₂" label on the jar.
4. Test the hypothesis: place about a teaspoon of baking soda in the small cup. With the jar and the watch ready, add about a tablespoon of vinegar in the small cup with the baking soda.
5. Quickly place the jar over both the small cup and the burning candle.
6. Record how many seconds it takes for the flame to go out. (It may only take 1 or 2 seconds.)
7. Was your hypothesis correct? Combustion reactions produce carbon dioxide, so adding more carbon dioxide does not help the flame burn. In fact, CO_2 extinguishes the flame.
8. After the flame goes out, clear the carbon dioxide out of the jar by blowing into it several times or rinsing it with water. Rinse and dry the small cup for the next reaction.

CANDLE PLUS OXYGEN GAS (O₂) UNDER A JAR:

[Note: follow this procedure exactly as it is essential that the oxygen burn as it is formed.]

1. Light the candle.
2. Form a hypothesis: will the flame burn longer or shorter if oxygen gas is added to the jar?
3. Place the "O₂" label on the jar.
4. Test the hypothesis: place about a teaspoon of baker's yeast in the small cup. With the jar and the watch ready, add about 3 tablespoons of hydrogen peroxide in the small cup with the baker's yeast.
5. Quickly place the jar over both the small cup and the burning candle.
6. Record how many seconds it takes for the flame to go out.
7. Was your hypothesis correct? Combustion reactions require oxygen gas, so adding more oxygen gas helps the flame burn longer.

- Look for combustion reactions as you go through your day (candle, gas stove, car engine, fire place, camp fire, etc). Review the rules of a combustion reaction every time your child identifies a combustion reaction.

APPLY IT

- Discuss various facets of the story of Shadrach, Meshach, and Abednego. Encourage your children to be brave for God.

Study how carbon dioxide is produced by combustion in our industrial plants and cars. Learn about the green house effect and climate change caused by too much carbon dioxide in our atmosphere.

GO BEYOND

PLANT REQUIREMENTS

Experiment with bean sprouts to determine what a plant needs to survive.

MATERIALS

1. 10-12 bean seeds.
2. Five 12-16 ounce plastic cups (use a sharp object to create a small hole in the bottom of each cup, and label them individually: "no soil", "no water", "no sun", and "no carbon dioxide", and "control").
3. Soil.
4. Water.
5. Tablespoon.
6. Gallon size plastic bag.
7. Dark place or painted out jar.

God created different plants to live all over the world. Where are some places you have seen plants? Did you know that some plants even grow in lakes and oceans? Did you know some plants even grow through the snow? What kinds of plants live in a desert?

BIG IDEA

In Matthew 13:1-8 Jesus tells us the Parable of the Sower. Listen carefully for where the seeds fell and what happened to the plants. (Students may wish to draw four pictures of the four plantings as the parable is read.) "Jesus went out of the house and sat by the lake. Such large crowds gathered around him that he got into a boat and sat in it, while all the people stood on the shore. Then he told them many things in parables, saying: "A farmer went out to sow his seed. As he was scattering the seed some fell along the path. The birds came and ate it up. Some fell on rocky places, where it did not have much soil. It sprang up quickly, because the soil was shallow. But when the sun came up, the plants were scorched, and they withered because they had no root. Other seed fell among thorns, which grew up and choked the plants. Still other seed fell on good soil, where it produced a crop—a hundred, sixty or thirty times what was sown.""

Matthew 13:9 "Whoever has ears, let them hear."

Jesus intended his audience to be very familiar with what a plant needs to survive. Many people had gardens and farms. Imagine that you are the farmer, planting the seeds that are the Word of God.

PLANT REQUIREMENTS

- The seeds that fell on the path were eaten by birds. This story shows what it is like if you tell someone about God, but Satan snatches the message away from their hearts before they have time to consider the truths in the Word.

- The seeds that fell on the rocky places did not have soil. These seeds did not have good roots to get water when the sun became hot. This is like what happens to people who hear the Word, but then fall away from God when it becomes too difficult to maintain their faith.

- The seeds that fell among the thorns and were choked. This story represents people who initially seem to be following Jesus, but the worries and activities in life choke their faith.

- The seeds that fell on good soil and produced a good crop. These people hear the Word, take it into their hearts, let it take root, nourish their faith, and do the good work God has planned for them.

How can you be like the seed that fell on good soil? How can you nourish your faith? (Read the Bible, make good friends, have quiet time, pray, obey God's commands, go to church, etc.)

Today we are going to learn what plants need to live. What do you think all plants need to live?

Let's experiment with what a plant might need to survive. God is not in a hurry, so it will take several days to learn what plants need. Can you be a patient learner?

ACTIVITIES

ACTIVITY 1

DO PLANTS NEED SOIL?

1. Set the "no soil" cup aside. Fill the 4 other cups about 3/4 full of soil.

2. Place 2-3 beans in each cup, including the "no soil" cup.

3. Form a hypothesis: Will the seeds in the "no soil" cup thrive?

ACTIVITY 2

DO PLANTS NEED WATER?

1. Set the "no water" cup aside. Add 2 tablespoons of water to the other 4 cups.

2. Form a hypothesis: Will the seeds in the "no water" cup thrive?

ACTIVITY 3

DO PLANTS NEED SUN?

1. Place the "no sun" cup in a dark room or dark jar (make sure the lid is loose).

2. Place the other 4 cups in a sunny window.

3. Form a hypothesis: Will the seeds in the "no sun" cup thrive?

PLANT REQUIREMENTS

LUNAR CRATERS

Understand the general texture of the surface of the moon. Experiment with creating craters in a false lunar surface. Define the parts of a crater.

BIG IDEA

MATERIALS

Genesis 1:1-5 tells us that:

In the beginning God created the heavens and the earth. Now the earth was formless and empty, darkness was over the surface of the deep, and the Spirit of God was hovering over the waters. And God said, "Let there be light," and there was light. God saw that the light was good, and he separated the light from the darkness. God called the light "day," and the darkness he called "night." And there was evening, and there was morning—the first day.

Genesis 1: 14-19 continues:

And God said, "Let there be lights in the vault of the sky to separate the day from the night, and let them serve as signs to mark sacred times, and days and years, and let them be lights in the vault of the sky to give light on the earth."And it was so. God made two great lights—the greater light to govern the day and the lesser light to govern the night. He also made the stars. God set them in the vault of the sky to give light on the earth, to govern the day and the night, and to separate light from darkness. And God saw that it was good. And there was evening, and there was morning—the fourth day.

1. Picture(s) of a lunar crater.

2. Large flat tub or box (about 1 ft by 1 ft, about 6 inches deep).

3. Enough flour to make a two inch deep layer in the bottom of the box (about 5 pounds).

4. One ruler per child,

5. Five small balls of various sizes and densities (golf ball, foam ball, baseball, marble etc).

6. A meter stick.

- What is the "darkness"?
    Night time, outer space, maybe black holes.

- What are the "lights" that separate day from night?
    The sun and the moon.

- What do you think the "heavens" include?
    How about stars, planets, nebula, asteroids, comets, galaxies? What else?

LUNAR CRATERS

When God was creating our solar system, our planet, and our moon, it was probably pretty exciting. There were lots of rocks and debris hurling through space. Many of these rocks smashed into the new planets and moons in our solar system. This was all part of God's plan as He beautifully molded our universe. Have you ever noticed how beautiful the moon is?

Here on Earth we have lots of rain, ice, and wind, so most of the marks left by the collisions during creation have been erased by our weather. However, the moon does not have weather. Therefore, the marks left by the collisions on the moon are still visible today!

Show the children the picture of the lunar crater. Did you know that up close, the surface of the moon looks like this? What shape is this? Can you see any shadows? What do the edges of the crater look like?

God made the moon with all of those bumps and craters on purpose. And it is good. God does not do anything by accident. God knows all about His creations. He even knows everything about you! Psalm 139:1–6 says:

> You have searched me, LORD,
> and you know me.
> You know when I sit and when I rise;
> you perceive my thoughts from afar.
> You discern my going out and my lying down;
> you are familiar with all my ways.
>
> Before a word is on my tongue
> you, Lord, know it completely.
> You hem me in behind and before,
> and you lay your hand upon me.
> Such knowledge is too wonderful for me,
> too lofty for me to attain.

Everything that God created is wonderful. And that means that God thinks you are wonderful!

What is one thing you think is really wonderful about yourself?
Is there anything you don't think is wonderful about yourself?

God created ALL of you, even the parts that you may not like. Do you think we should thank God for his wonderful creation? Take a moment for a prayer of thanksgiving. Let the children take turns praising God for what is wonderful about them.

LUNAR CRATERS

Lunar Craters

[best if done outside, can be messy]

1. Pour the flour into the bottom of the box. Ask the students to use their rulers to help smooth the flour (not pack). Explain that the surface of the moon is very soft and dusty like flour.

2. Have each student pick a ball (impactor) to drop.

3. Hold the meter stick upright just inside the edge of the box of flour.

4. Form a hypothesis: What will happen to the surface of the flour if an impactor is dropped from the height of the meter stick?

5. Test the hypothesis: Ask the child to drop, not throw, the impactor from the height of the meter stick directly down into the flour.

    a. Does this crater look like the ones on the moon? How is it similar? How is it different? One major difference is that the impactor is present in the model, while it disintegrates upon impact on the moon.

    b. Do you notice any ejecta (loose material thrown out of the crater)?

    c. Do you notice any rays (long streaks extending out from the crater)?

6. Let the children take turns experimenting with various impactors. Form a hypothesis each time a new impactor is presented.

7. Form a hypothesis: What will happen if an impactor is dropped from half way up the meter stick?

8. Test the hypothesis. Older children can use a ruler to measure crater depth and width, comparing it to that of the same impactor dropped from the top of the meter stick.

9. Let the children design an experiment, form a hypothesis, test the hypothesis, and draw a conclusion.

10. Drop an impactor to form a nice crater in deep flour. Point out the following parts. Older children can create a labeled drawing.

    a. Floor – bottom of the crater.

    b. Walls – inside steep grade of the crater. Gravity often causes them to cave and slump.

    c. Rim – edge of the crater. It is pushed up upon impact.

    d. Ejecta – material thrown out of the crater in the near vicinity of the crater.

    e. Rays – bright streaks extending away from the crater. These can travel great distances.

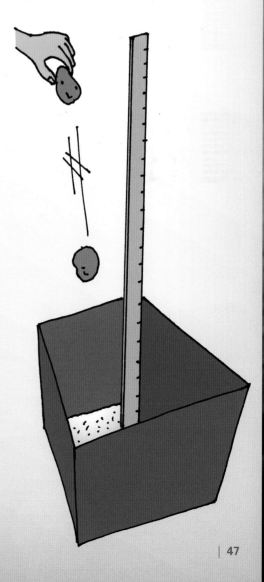

God Knows You

1. Prior to the lesson, secretly attain the answers to the following questions from three or four people with whom the students are familiar. You can ask students, family members, or teachers.

   a. If you had a dog, what would you name it?

   b. What is your favorite dessert?

   c. What is your favorite thing about school?

   d. If you were going to be a Bible character, who would it be?

2. Ask the children if they know each other? It is important to take time to get to know people, although we can never know as much as God. How does it feel when someone cares about you and pays attention to you? How does it feel to be ignored? If you ever feel lonely, remember that God loves you and really knows you.

3. This activity will help you know each other more. Read one set of answers to the secret questions. Ask the children to guess who fits the description. If they cannot guess, reveal the correct answers.

4. Re-read Psalm 139:1-6. Ask the children to point out all that God knows.

5. God knows all about the good parts and the bad parts of each of you. And he still loves you. That is wonderful.

APPLY IT

- Are there things about yourself that you do not like? Do you think that if the moon had feelings it would "like" having all of those craters? If you do not like the color of your hair, how tall you are, or the size of your feet, remember Psalm 139:1. God knows everything about you and still loves you. Give God praise for all of His creation.

- If your child sees a shooting star, explain that it is actually a tiny piece of space debris left over from God's creation so many years ago. The tiny meteor burns up in Earth's atmosphere, creating a streak of light. These meteors are far too small to leave any craters.

- Study the Barringer Meteor Crater in Arizona.

LUNAR CRATERS

- Study Galileo's contributions to astronomy. (See page 92). He was the first person to use the word "crater".

- Look at a quarter moon (when half is showing) with a telescope or good pair of binoculars. Can you see any crater marks? The quarter moon is a good phase for viewing craters because shadows are cast across the crater, better defining the features.

GO BEYOND

Experiment 11:

WATER CYCLE

Understand evaporation and condensation. Explore the phase changes of water. Learn the basic water cycle.

MATERIALS

1. Large clear bowl.
2. Small yogurt cup with the top inch cut off the edge.
3. Big rubber band to go around the top of the bowl.
4. Two weights or smooth rocks small enough to fit into the yogurt cup.
5. Plastic wrap.

BIG IDEA

Have you ever prayed earnestly for something important?

Has it ever seemed as if **God** was not answering?

Have you ever wondered if **God** heard your prayer or cared about your requests?

At these times you may doubt if God's promises are true. There is great news for us: the Bible is clear that all of God's promises are true.

2 Corinthians 1:20 says,

> **"No matter how many promises God has made, they are 'Yes' in Christ."**

Sometimes this may not seem true to us because we do not know God's perfect plan, but God always keeps His promises for His people. It may not be the way we would do it. It may not be the time we think we want it. Be encouraged to keep praying, trusting in God's promises. God does all things in His way at His time.

Zechariah 10:1 says "Ask the LORD for rain in the springtime; it is the LORD who sends the thunderstorms. He gives showers of rain to all people, and plants of the field to everyone."

What is the promise in this verse?

Why do humans need water?

Why do plants and animals need water?

Every human, plant, and animal requires water to live. The water on our planet is constantly being cleaned and replenished through the water cycle. (Ask more advanced students to draw and label a diagram of the elements of the water cycle as you explain.)

- The sun shines on the lakes, oceans, and puddles. The water gets warm and evaporates. It changes from a liquid water to a gas called water vapor.

WATER CYCLE

- Trees drink water through their roots. The water travels up the trunk and to the leaves. When it reaches the leaves, it exits the tree and transpires as water vapor.

- Even in cold places, snow sublimates by changing directly from solid snowflakes into water vapor.

- Once all of the water vapor is floating around, it begins to rise up, up, up ... As it rises, it gets cooler and cooler. Cool water vapor condenses and changes back into tiny liquid water particles to form a cloud.

- More and more water vapor condenses in the clouds. The water droplets in the clouds grow larger and larger. When the droplets get large enough, the winds in the cloud can no longer hold them up, and they precipitate from the sky. Precipitation is the word for rain, snow, sleet, or hail.

The Lord has control over all forces of nature and can use them for His purposes. The following story is an example of how the Lord uses the water cycle to bring his people back to Him. Listen for the ways God controls the water cycle.

1 Kings 17 and 18:

Elijah was a good prophet of the LORD who lived in Israel. But the people of Israel were being lead by a King Ahab and Queen Jezebel. And they did not love the LORD or follow his commands; they followed false gods called Baals. Even though they were misbehaving, God still loved His children, and wanted them to love Him. So just as a parent punishes a child who disobeys, God sent punishment to the people of Israel for breaking the rules. God instructed Elijah to tell everyone that there would be a drought; "there will be neither dew nor rain in the next few years except at my word." This was really bad news. Because if there is no rain, what happens to the plants? If there are no plants what happens to the animals? If there are no plants or animals, what happens to the people?

The LORD took care of Elijah, and commanded him to hide in a rocky place in the mountains. God knew Ahab and Jezebel would be furious about the drought and would want to hurt Elijah for bringing God's message. God provided water for Elijah from a little stream. And God provided food for Elijah by commanding ravens to bring him meat and bread. But the drought was so bad, that the little stream dried up. However, God took care of Elijah again, and told him to go to stay with a widow in a nearby town. Everyone was hungry and thirsty because there had been no rain. When Elijah asked her for food and water, she said, "As surely as the LORD your God lives, I don't have any bread—only a handful of flour in a jar and a little olive oil in a jug. I am gathering a few sticks to take home and make a meal for myself and my son, that we may eat it—and die." Elijah said to her, "Don't be afraid ... make a small loaf of bread for me from what you have and bring it to me, and then make something for yourself and your son. For this is what the LORD, the God of Israel, says: 'The jar of flour will not be used up and the jug of oil will not run dry until the day the LORD sends rain on the land." And it was true. Every day, the woman made bread, but she did not run out of oil and flour.

Three years passed. Finally, God commanded Elijah to go see King Ahab. By this time, people were really hungry and thirsty. Everybody was looking for food and water, even King Ahab. He sent a man named Obadiah to find green grass for his cows and horses. Elijah meet Obadiah, and told him he would like to see King Ahab. When King Ahab showed up, he blamed Elijah for the drought. But, Elijah spoke the truth and said, "I have not made trouble for Israel. But you and your father's family have. You have abandoned the LORD's commands and have followed the Baals."

WATER CYCLE

Elijah wanted to show everyone how powerful God was so they would stop following the false gods. So he called a meeting on Mount Carmel and invited four hundred and fifty prophets of Baal. Elijah challenged them to a contest.

He said, "I am the only one of the LORD's prophets left, but Baal has four hundred and fifty prophets. Get two bulls for us. Let Baal's prophets choose one for themselves, and let them cut it into pieces and put it on the wood but not set fire to it. I will prepare the other bull and put it on the wood but not set fire to it. Then you call on the name of your god, and I will call on the name of the LORD. The god who answers by fire—he is God." The prophets of Baal accepted the challenge, killed a bull, cut it up, put it on the pile of wood, and prayed to Baal to send fire. Those prophets danced and screamed and shouted to Baal all day long. What do you think happened? Do you think Baal sent fire? Of course not. Because they were praying to someone who does not even exist. When the prophets were completely worn out from all of their frantic praying, Elijah gathered everyone around. He used twelve stones to rebuild the alter of the LORD, which had been torn down. Then he dug a ditch around the alter, like a moat around a castle. He put the wood on the alter, killed a bull, cut it into pieces, and laid them on the wood. Then Elijah did something that must have seemed very wasteful and foolish, considering the drought. He soaked the offering with jar after jar full of precious water. The meat was wet. The wood was wet. The stones were wet. The ground was wet. Even the ditch was full of water. Is it easy to set something on fire that is soaking wet? Then Elijah stepped forward and prayed, "LORD, the God of Abraham, Isaac and Israel, let it be known today that you are God in Israel and that I am your servant and have done all these things at your command. Answer me, LORD, answer me, so these people will know that you, LORD, are God, and that you are turning their hearts back again." Then fire fell from the sky and burned up the bull, the wood, the stones, the soil, and even licked up the water in the ditch. When the people saw this, they were amazed and cried out, "The LORD – he is God!"

Then Elijah said to Ahab, "Go, eat and drink, for there is the sound of a heavy rain." So Ahab went off to eat and drink, but Elijah climbed to the top of Carmel to pray for rain. He sent his servant to go look toward the sea seven times. The seventh time, the servant reported, "A cloud as small as a man's hand is rising from the sea."

So Elijah said, "Go and tell Ahab, 'Hitch up your chariot and go down before the rain stops you.'" And the sky grew black with clouds, the wind rose, a heavy rain started falling. Ahab got in his chariot to ride home in the pouring rain. The power of the LORD came on Elijah. He tucked his cloak into his belt and ran so fast, that he outran the horses pulling Ahab's chariot.

WATER CYCLE

WATER CYCLE MODEL

ACTIVITY 1

1. Place the trimmed yogurt cup in the center of the large bowl.

2. Place one rock or weight in the yogurt cup.

3. Add water to the bottom of the large bowl, making sure not to fill the yogurt cup. Do not add so much water that the yogurt cup floats.

4. Cover the bowl with plastic wrap, and secure it around the edge with a rubber band. It is best if you can leave a little slack in the plastic wrap over the bowl, but still seal it securely around the edges.

5. Place a weight or rock on the center top of the plastic wrap so that it creates a downward slant over the yogurt cup.

6. Carefully place the whole thing in a warm sunny place. Do not let water splash into the yogurt cup.

7. Form a hypothesis:
   What will happen to the water in the bowl?

8. Check on the bowl every thirty minutes until results are visible.

9. The heat from the sun makes the water in the big bowl evaporate. The water vapor then rises to the top where it condenses on the cooler plastic wrap. It runs toward the weight to drip off into the yogurt cup like precipitation.

THE WATER CYCLE POEM:

ACTIVITY 2

Make up hand motions while reciting this rhythmic poem.

Trees transpire
and snow sublimates.

For the water cycle
that's what it takes.

Lakes evaporate
and clouds condensate.

Then it all comes together
to precipitate.

GOD PROMISES RAIN

ACTIVITY 3

Read the following verses and find the phrases that promise rain.

Why was/is rain so important?

1. Isaiah 30:23

2. Jeremiah 10:13

3. Joel 2:23

4. Psalm 135:7

WATER CYCLE

Do Plants Need Carbon Dioxide?

1. Place the "no carbon dioxide" cup in the air tight plastic baggie (in the sunny place). Press as much air out of the bag as possible and seal it securely. Remind the students that the bag keeps air from flowing to and from the plant. It also inhibits evaporation of the water.

2. Form a hypothesis: Will the seeds in the "no carbon dioxide" cup thrive?

3. Note that the "control" cup has everything: soil, water, sun, and carbon dioxide.

4. Check on the plants in two days. What do you observe? Add 2 tablespoons of water to the soil of the 4 cups which receive water if the soil is dry to the touch. The "no carbon dioxide" cup will probably NOT need water because the plastic bag prevents water from escaping.

5. Check on the plants again in two more days. Add water again if needed.

6. Within about two weeks major differences in plant growth will be evident.

7. Discuss the visible differences in plant development.
   Ask older children to record the results.

APPLY IT

- Look around for plants that are unhealthy. Discuss why they might not be thriving. For house plants over watering is often a problem; this is a good opportunity to teach the children that plants need just the right amount of water.

- Recall the four types of seed plantings as described in the Parable of the Sower. What important component were the plants missing?

  o The seeds that <u>fell on the path</u> were eaten by birds. They did not have time to make roots.

  o The seeds that <u>fell on the rocky places</u> did not have soil. They did not grow good roots, so they could not absorb water.

  o The seeds that <u>fell among the thorns</u> were choked. The thorns shaded the seeds, so they did not have enough sunlight. The thorns also soaked the water from the soil.

  o The seeds that <u>fell on good soil</u> produced a good crop. These seeds had water, sunlight, carbon dioxide, and good soil.

GO BEYOND

- Have older children record plant growth data for each of the five cups. They can then create a line graph to plot plant growth over time, such that the x axis is days and the y axis is plant height.

- Repeat the experiment, but allow the seedlings to sprout and grow about three inches tall before exposing them to the variable conditions. Do the results change? How?

MORE SCIENCE:

TURGOR PRESSURE

A plant cell is constructed like a balloon full of water, blown up tight inside a cardboard box. Note: you may wish to build and label this model plant cell. The cardboard box is like the cell wall, and the balloon is like the cell membrane. The plant is constructed of many plant cells stacked together. The pressure created by water inside plant cells is called turgor pressure. Water moves through the cell membrane of plant cell walls by a process called osmosis. If there is not enough water inside the cell membrane, the cell becomes soft; the balloons deflate and the boxes collapse. This makes the plant appear wilted. When there is plenty of water, plants maintain good turgor pressure; the balloons are filled and the boxes stacked tight. The plant cells are firm and healthy, the stems are rigid and leaves opened.

So, next time there is dry weather, and you notice that the plants are wilted, you might say, "Sure is dry. All of my plants are losing turgor pressure."

PHOTOSYNTHESIS

This word is hard to say, but easy to understand. "Photo" is Greek for "light," and "synthesis" is Greek for "put together." So do you know what photosynthesis means for plants? They use light to put things together! Specifically, they use light to put together their own food. In order to perform this amazing process, plants need carbon dioxide, water, and sunlight. Carbon dioxide is abundant in our atmosphere. You exhale it with every breath. Water is found in the ground. The roots bring the water up to the stem, and to the leaves. This maintains good turgor pressure.

Carbon Dioxide + Water + Light → Sugar (plant food) + Oxygen

When you breathe, you use oxygen and have carbon dioxide waste. But God created a wonderful balance. When plants breathe, they use carbon dioxide and create oxygen as waste. So what would happen to your breathing if all of the plants were gone?

Plant cells contain tiny chloroplasts. They make the leaves green, and they perform the photosynthesis by using carbon dioxide, water, and light to make sugars and oxygen. So if you were a plant, and you were hungry, all you need to do is take a deep breath, drink a big glass of water, and go stand out in the sun. You would make your own tasty snack.

PLANT REQUIREMENTS

- Notice elements of the water cycle in the weather: rain, snow, humidity, cloud formations, shrinking puddles, tree leaves, etc. Any time it rains, remind the children that God keeps His promises.

- Study the story of Joseph's dream in Genesis 37:1-9. Then trace the series of events that unfold to fulfill this promise. Genesis 37:10-36 and Genesis 39–42.

- What does the Bible tell us about taking care of the earth in Genesis 2:15? Study the life of Lynn Townsend White Jr., one of the first Christian conservationists. (See page 95).

GO BEYOND

EVAPORATION AND TEMPERATURE

1. Place 10 ml (2 teaspoons) of water in each of two identical saucers. Place one saucer in the sunlight or under a close, warm light source.

2. Place the other saucer in the shade.

3. Form a hypothesis: Which saucer's water will evaporate faster?

4. Observe each dish after four hours, then again the next day. Record observations.

5. From which saucer did the water evaporate faster? Why? Where did the water go?

WATER USAGE

1. Find the water meter for your house or school.

2. Write the reading down at the same time every day for a week. The water meter may record gallons or cubic feet of water.

3. Subtract each day's reading from the next day's reading to determine daily usage.

4. If you want to convert cubic feet into gallons, multiply each cubic foot reading by 7.5 to change your data to gallons.

5. Create a graph showing water usage. The Y axis is gallons (or cubic feet) and the X axis is days.

CONSERVING WATER

1. Brainstorm ways your family can save water.

   a. Here are a few ideas to help get you started:

      i. Inside: fix drippy faucets, turn off the water after you wet your toothbrush, turn off the shower water while soaping up then turn it back on to rinse, run only full loads in the dishwasher and washing machine.

      ii. Outside: place mulch around shrubs and garden plants so the ground around their roots retains water, use sprinklers in the morning or evening to minimize evaporation, plant drought resistant gardens.

2. Put the ideas into action for one month.

3. Compare your water bill to see if it is lower than the water bill from the same month of the previous year.

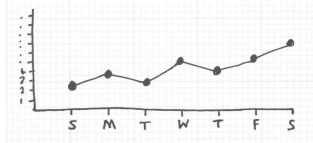

ANGLE OF THE SUN'S RAYS

Understand that the sun's rays warm the surface of our earth.
Record data for the temperature change over the course of a day
(sunny spring and fall days have the most notable change).
Create a line graph and interpret the data collected.

MATERIALS

1. Small bouncy ball.

2. An easy to read thermometer (Celsius or Fahrenheit).

3. An easy to read clock (optional).

4. Graph paper.

[Hazards: Never look straight at the sun.]

"... God made two great lights; the greater light to rule the day, and the lesser light to rule the night..." Genesis 1:16 (NKJV)

BIG IDEA

What do you think these two great lights are?
God created the sun and the moon! What
are some things the sun gives us? (light, warmth, photosynthesis). Can
you imagine what our world would be like without a sun? (dark and cold).

Here is a story from Joshua 10 about God's amazing power over the sun.
Joshua was the leader of the people of Israel. He was a warrior for the
LORD, commanding men and fighting to take the promised land for the
people of Israel. Joshua was winning a lot of battles, marching his way
across the land. Five of the kings who lived there heard of how well Joshua
and the Israelite warriors were doing. They were worried that he would
conquer their cities too. So they decided to join forces and attack the
city of Gibeon because this city had made a peace treaty with Israel. The
Gibeonites were not happy about being attacked, so they sent a message
to Joshua, "Do not abandon your servants. Come up to us quickly and save
us! Help us, because all the Amorite kings from the hill country have joined
forces against us."

Now Joshua was so determined to get to Gibeon and
help, he marched all night long with his entire army,
including all the best fighting men. The LORD said to
Joshua, "Do not be afraid of them; I have given
them into your hand. Not one of them will be able to
withstand you."

Joshua and his warriors caught the five kings and their armies

ANGLE OF SUN'S RAYS

BIG IDEA CONTINUED...

off guard, fought and won the battle, and then chased all day after the enemy soldiers who ran away from the battle. But the sun was setting, and Joshua had not yet killed every last foe. So he prayed:

"Sun, stand still over Gibeon,
and you, moon, over the Valley of Aijalon."

So the sun stood still, and the moon stopped. The sun stopped right in the middle of the sky and did not set until the next day. The Bible says there has never been a day like this before or since. Surely the LORD was fighting for Israel!

Since God made the sun and the moon, He controls everything about the sun and the moon. When they rise, when they set, how hot they shine, how bright they shine. God created such a wonderful sun to give light and warmth to our planet. Today, we are going to take notice of how much heat the sun gives our earth.

ACTIVITY 1

"STAND STILL"

1. Ask the children to stand up and run in place. Tell them to freeze when the teacher says "stand still" and resume moving when the teacher says "go". Continue alternating until attention spans wane.

2. God is completely in control of everything! He even controls the rising and setting of the sun.

ANGLE OF THE SUN'S RAYS

ACTIVITY 2

1. The sun's warming rays hit our part of the planet more directly during the middle of the day, giving us more heat. Therefore, it is warmer! Use a small bouncy ball to demonstrate how a sun's ray would hit our planet directly by bouncing the ball straight down onto the table/floor.

"hotter"

2. But in the morning and the evening, the sun's rays hit our part of the planet at an angle, giving us less heat. Therefore, it is cooler! Use a small bouncy ball to demonstrate how a sun's ray would hit our planet at an angle by bouncing the ball diagonally across the table/floor.

"cooler"

3. Allow the students to bounce the ball saying "hotter" for the direct bounces and "cooler" for the angular bounces.

COLLECTING DATA

ACTIVITY 3

Best if done on a sunny day. This can take as much or as little time as the teacher chooses, but at least three temperatures need to be recorded: morning, noon, and evening.

1. In the morning hours, read the thermometer. For more advanced students, have them record the time and temperature. For younger students, have them record the "morning" temperature. Make sure you use the same scale all day, either Celsius or Fahrenheit.

2. Advanced students can record the temperature every hour throughout the day. It is helpful if they write the times down first, then record the temperatures when the time comes. Younger students can simply record the morning, noon, and evening (or breakfast, lunch, and dinner) temperatures.

ACTIVITY 4

LINE GRAPH

1. Help the students draw a horizontal "X" axis labeled "Time." Advanced students can write the times across the X axis; younger students can simply write "morning" on the left, "noon" in the center, and "evening" on the right.

2. And a vertical "Y" axis labeled "Temperature". Help your students correctly label the Y axis such that the lowest number is approximately that of the lowest recorded temperature, the highest number is approximately that of the highest recorded temperature, and the resulting intervals are evenly spaced.

3. Plot the points on the graph. It should create a mountain shape.

4. Study the graph together. Then ask:

    a. What time was it hottest today? Why?

    b. What time was it coolest today? Why?

    c. Why is the graph this shape?

    d. What do you think a graph of tonight's temperatures would look like?

    e. What do you think a graph of tomorrow's temperatures would look like?

- When your child is dressing warmly in the morning, remind him that the sun's rays are hitting the earth at an indirect angle, so it is going to be cool. When you notice your child removing his coat as the day warms up, remind him that the angle of the sun's rays is becoming more direct.

APPLY IT

- Use construction paper, scissors, and markers to creatively create a sun and a moon. Write the first part of Genesis 1:16 on the sun "God made two great lights; the greater light to rule the day." And write the second part of Genesis 1:16 (NKJV) on the moon "and the lesser light to rule the night." Place these in a prominent place where children can readily review the memory verse.

ANGLE OF SUN'S RAYS

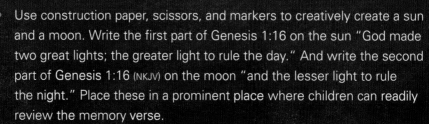

- Read the story of the crucifixion of Christ in Mark 15.

  What happened to the sun?
  Why do you think God did this?

- Use the data you collected in Activity 2 to create a graph in excel or a similar computer program.
- Collect temperature data on vernal equinox, summer solstice, fall equinox, and winter solstice. Create graphs and compare the data.

ANGLE OF SUN'S RAYS

ANGLE OF A FLASHLIGHT

Explore how the angle of a light affects temperature.

ACTIVITY

MATERIALS

1. Sheet of black paper.
2. Alcohol weather thermometer.
3. Flashlight.
4. Ruler.
5. Tape.
6. Clock or watch.

Procedure:

1. Lay the thermometer on the black paper.
2. Tape the ruler to the underside of the flashlight so that six inches is sticking out from the lighted end. This will hold the flashlight 6 inches from the thermometer, even when the angle changes.
3. Shine the beam directly down on the thermometer for five minutes.
4. Record the temperature.
5. Let the thermometer return to approximately room temperature.
6. Form a hypothesis: will the temperature increase or decrease if the flashlight is held at an angle?
7. Test the hypothesis: Hold the flashlight at approximately a 45° angle, keeping it six inches from the thermometer for five minutes.
8. Record the temperature.

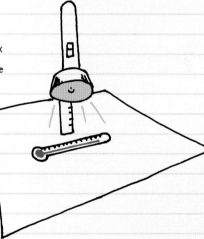

Which angle had the higher temperature?

Do the sun's rays hit the earth directly or at an angle in the summer?

What about in the winter?

Experiment 13:

BASIC ANIMAL CLASSIFICATION

Understand the characteristics of the five basic classes of animals.
Be introduced to the concept of species classification.

MATERIALS

1. 4 x 6 note cards (5 per child).
2. Old magazines, news papers. calendars, etc.
5. Scissors.
6. Glue sticks.

God made so many different kinds of living things... What are some living things that you can think of? Make sure examples of the five kingdoms are mentioned: plants, animals, fungi, monera (bacteria), and protists (protozoa and algae).

BIG IDEA

God made so many living creatures, it is difficult for people to keep up with all of them. So scientists invented a way to classify living things into categories according to how they are similar and how they are different. Today, we are going to study the <u>animal kingdom, chordata phylum</u> (which simply means animals that have a backbone).

There are five different classes of animals in this phylum. Do you want to guess them? Name some animals. When the children name an animal such as "frog", say "good, that's an amphibian." If the child says "shark" say "good, that's a fish."

1. <u>Mammals</u>: give birth to live babies, have hair or fur, mothers nurse their babies with milk, warm blooded. People are mammals.

2. <u>Birds</u>: have feathers and wings (but may not fly), lay hard shelled eggs, warm blooded.

3. <u>Reptiles</u>: have scales and dry skin, usually lay firm shelled eggs (sometimes give live birth to babies), cold blooded.

4. <u>Amphibians</u>: live on land and in the water, lay jelly sack eggs, slimy wet skin, webbed feet.

5. <u>Fish</u>: breathe under water with gills, have scales or smooth skin, cold blooded, lay eggs.

ANIMAL CLASSIFICATION

God Created the Animals

ACTIVITY 1

1. Get the children to listen for all of these types of animals in Genesis 1:20-25. Read over the following verses several times until the children understand the various types of animals mentioned.

And God said, "Let the water teem with living creatures, and let <u>birds</u> fly above the earth across the vault of the sky." So God created the great <u>creatures of the sea</u> and every living thing with which the water teems and that moves about in it, according to their kinds, and every <u>winged bird</u> according to its kind. And God saw that it was good. God blessed them and said, "Be fruitful and increase in number and fill the water in the seas, and let the <u>birds</u> increase on the earth." And there was evening, and there was morning – the fifth day. And God said, "Let the land produce living creatures according to their kinds: the <u>livestock, the creatures that move along the ground</u>, and the <u>wild animals</u>, each according to its kind." And it was so.

> **Genesis 1:25: God made the wild animals according to their kinds, the livestock according to their kinds, and all the creatures that move along the ground according to their kinds. And God saw that it was good.**

2. Mammals – "livestock" (domestic horses, cows, donkeys, goats, etc.), "wild animals".

3. Birds – "let birds fly above the earth across the vault of the sky", "wild animals".

4. Reptiles – "the creatures that move along the ground", "wild animals".

5. Amphibians – "the creatures that move along the ground", "wild animals".

6. Fish – "the great creatures of the sea", "wild animals".

Animal Classification Cards

ACTIVITY 2

1. Ask the children to write one animal class on each of their cards.

2. Older children can also write the characteristics listed above. Younger children can simply review the characteristics while they write.

3. Give each child a magazine, ask them to find any animals and cut them out.

   - Remember, insects do not have a backbone. Insects and spiders are in phylum arthropoda, not phylum chordate. They are only searching for chordates, animals with a backbone.

   - Humans are mammals, but are listed separately in the story of creation.

   - Where an animal lives is not necessarily an indicator of which class it is in. For instance, the ocean is full of fish, but dolphins and whales are mammals. The air is full of birds, but bats are mammals.

4. Then glue the cut out animals to the correct card; use front and back of the card. Allow the children to label and glue more cards if they wish.

5. The cards can be studied and added to for weeks.

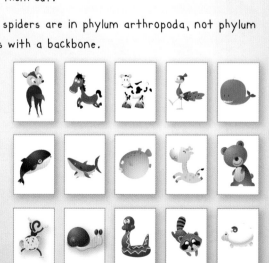

- As you go through your week, point out the class of animals that you see. Also recall on which day of creation God made them – Birds and fish were created on day 5. Mammals, reptiles, and amphibians were created on day 6, as were humans.

- Play animal charades. One student stands before the class and mimics an animal of his/her choosing without words (animal sounds are optional). When a student correctly guesses the animal, he/she must also classify it and identify which day it was created by God.

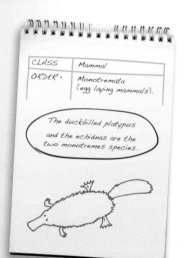

CLASS	Mammal
ORDER·	Monotremata (egg laying mammals).

The duckbilled platypus and the echidnas are the two monotremes species.

Ask students to guess how to classify the duckbilled platypus.

It lays eggs, has a bill, and has webbed feet. But it has fur. What is it?

- Class: Mammal,

- Order: Monotremata (egg laying mammals).

The duckbilled platypus and the echidnas are the two monotremes species.

GO BEYOND

Create a Venn diagram to compare and contrast two animal classes.

- Draw two large circles that overlap about half of their size. Make the circles large enough to fill a piece of paper. Over one circle write "reptiles". Over the other circle write "mammals". Write details that tell how the subjects are different in the outer circles. Write details that tell how the subjects are alike where the circles overlap.

- Repeat this activity using various animal classes.

Example:

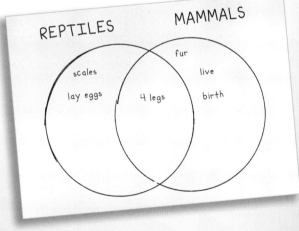

REPTILES   MAMMALS

scales   fur
lay eggs   4 legs   live birth

ANIMAL CLASSIFICATION

- Study the work of taxonomist Carolus Linnaeus. (See page 93) He created the modern scientific classification system.

- Further study the full system of animal classification: kingdom, phylum, class, order, family, genus, species. Make up memory scheme like, "keep ponds clean or fish get sick." Allow each student to choose one animal to research. Study the complete classification of that animal.

Animal Classification
Zoo Trip

Classify zoo animals according to scientific taxonomy.

BIG IDEA

Job 12:7-10 says, "But ask the beasts, and they will teach you; the birds of the heavens, and they will tell you; or the bushes of the earth, and they will teach you; and the fish of the sea will declare to you. Who among all these does not know that the hand of the LORD has done this [creation]?"

Job 12:10 – In his hand is the life of every living thing and the breath of all mankind. (ESV)

MATERIALS

1. 4 x 6 note cards (at least 5 per child).

2. A writing utensil for each child.

3. A zoo.

4. Binoculars (optional).

What does this passage mean? Even the birds, the beasts, the bushes, and the fish know who created them. In this passage, the living things not only know who created them, they also have a message for us.

- "But ask the beasts, and they will teach you".
- "the birds of the heavens ... will tell you".
- "the bushes of the earth ... will teach you".
- "the fish of the sea will declare to you".

By studying creation, we will inevitably learn more about the Creator. God created life and every living thing. Life is His speciality, and you are a masterpiece.

God's creatures are so beautiful and interesting. Let's take a closer look at some creatures in the <u>animal kingdom, chordate phylum</u>. Let's review the characteristics of the five classes in this phylum:

- <u>Mammals</u>: give birth to live babies, have hair or fur, mothers nurse their babies with milk, warm blooded. People are mammals.
- <u>Birds</u>: have feathers and wings (but may not fly), lay hard shelled eggs, warm blooded.
- <u>Reptiles</u>: have scales and dry skin, usually lay firm shelled eggs (sometimes give live birth to babies), cold blooded.
- <u>Amphibians</u>: live on land and in the water, lay jelly sack eggs, slimy wet skin, webbed feet.
- <u>Fish</u>: breathe under water with gills, have scales or smooth skin, cold blooded, lay eggs.

ZOO TRIP

Zoo Hunt

1. Ask the children to write one animal class on each of their cards.

2. Create a goal appropriate for your zoo and students' ages regarding how many of each animal to find. For instance, everyone needs to find ten mammals, ten birds, two reptiles, two amphibians, and two fish. Have students number each of their cards so they know how many animals to search for.

3. If multiple parents or teachers are present, it may be fun to split into groups and compete.

4. Begin walking through the zoo. When the children take notice of a particular animal, determine its class. Clarify misconceptions as they arise.

5. Write the name of the animal on the correct classification card.

A Psalm of Praise

1. Are God's creatures wonderful? Which zoo animal did you like the most? Why did you like that animal?

Listen to what David had to say about creation from Psalm 145:8-13:

"The LORD is gracious and compassionate,
slow to anger and rich in love.
The LORD is good to all;
he has compassion on all he has made.
All your works praise you, LORD;
your faithful people extol you.

They tell of the glory of your kingdom
and speak of your might,
so that all people may know of your mighty acts
and the glorious splendor of your kingdom.
Your kingdom is an everlasting kingdom,
and your dominion endures through all generations."

2. Reread the passage four more times, each time searching for answers to the following questions:

- What are the characteristics of God? Gracious, compassionate, slow to anger, rich in love, good to all.

- What are the characteristics of His works? Praise Him, glorious Kingdom, everlasting Kingdom, dominion endures.

- What are the characteristics of His people? Faithful people extol (worship) Him, tell others of the glory of His kingdom, speak of His might (power).

- Is there a command in this passage? We are to worship God and tell others of his power. The beauty of creation is one of His most apparent miracles. Spread the word that God is creator of all things for all time.

ZOO TRIP

- Show and tell: Tell about your favorite animal in the chordate phylum. What class is it in?
- As you go through your week, point out the class of animals that you see.
- Read Psalm 145:3 – 7. What else did David mention about creation?

> **G**reat is the **L**ORD and most worthy of praise;
> his greatness no one can fathom.
> One generation commends your works to another;
> they tell of your mighty acts.
> They speak of the glorious splendor of your majesty—
> and I will meditate on your wonderful works.
> They tell of the power of your awesome works—
> and I will proclaim your great deeds.
> They celebrate your abundant goodness
> and joyfully sing of your righteousness.

ZOO TRIP

GO BEYOND

- Read the story of Noah's Ark in Genesis 5:32 through 8:22. Listen for various animals mentioned in this story. Just as we are descendants of Noah, all of the creatures alive on Earth today are descendents of those animals who rode in the ark. (Except for those animals that lived in the water.) God put a male and a female of each animal species in the ark so they could have babies and repopulate the whole planet.

- There may be animals at the zoo that are not in the chordate phylum, especially if there is an aquatic element or a butterfly garden. There are approximately 40 phyla in the animal kingdom. However, most animals fall into one of these five phyla:

  o Chordata – vertebrates
  o Cnidaria – coral, jelly fish, anemones
  o Arthropoda – insects, arachnids, and crustaceans
  o Mollusca – squid, octopus, snails, clams, and slugs
  o Echinodermata – starfish, sea urchins, sand dollars, and sea cucumbers.

Discuss the classification of creatures which are not chordates.

NERVOUS SYSTEM

Learn the main parts of the nervous system: brain, spinal cord, and peripheral nervous system. Study the structure and function of a neuron. Explore neural conduction.

MATERIALS

1. One note card for every child with a familiar location written on it (grocery store, Sunday school class, restaurant, movie theater, playground, etc.).

2. Paper bag.

3. Blindfold.

4. 8 x 10 full body photo of each child (to be used throughout the anatomy lessons).

5. Before the lesson cut out of a small gray/grey paper brain for each child to glue onto her photo, paper and pencil/markers.

Who made you? Who made all people? Who made everything? Listen to this amazing story from Genesis 1 and 2 of how God made the first people.

God worked for six days making light, day and night, water, land, sky, plants, sun, moon, stars, birds, fish, and all of the animals. The world was almost complete. But God still had one very important thing to create: people! In Genesis 1:26-27 God said, "'Let us make mankind in our image, in our likeness, so that they may rule over the fish in the sea and the birds in the sky, over the livestock and all the wild animals, and over all the creatures that move along the ground.' So God created mankind in his own image, in the image of God he created them; male and female he created them."

BIG IDEA

God created everything from nothing.

Do you know the first man's name? Adam! God made Adam in the most amazing way. He picked up a handful of dust from the ground and molded it into the shape of a man. Then God took a deep breath and breathed into the nose of Adam. But the breath of God is not ordinary breath. God breathed the breath of life, and the dust became a living man!

God put Adam in the beautiful Garden of Eden, a special place He had made for his children to live. Adam's job was to work in the garden and take care of it. He also gave Adam the super cool job of naming all of the creatures.

But God saw that something was missing. In Genesis 2:18 God said, "It is not good for the man to be alone. I will make a helper suitable for him."

NERVOUS SYSTEM

Who do you think this helper was? God put Adam into a deep, deep sleep. And while Adam was sleeping, God took out one of his ribs and healed the place where the rib had been. Then God made a woman from the rib. Do you know the first woman's name? Eve! Genesis 2:23 tells us that when Adam saw Eve, he said:

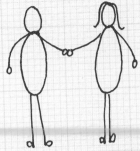

NERVOUS SYSTEM

"This is now bone of my bones

and flesh of my flesh;

she shall be called 'woman,'

for she was taken out of man."

God blessed Adam and Eve and told them to have lots of children. So they did. They had children, and their children had children, and their children's children had children, and their children's children's children had children. So that every single person on the Earth is the descendent of Adam and Eve. This includes you!

Although we are all part of the same family of humans, God made each person in the whole world special. There are unique differences in each person. How are you different from other people? How big you are. How you talk. How you move. What you are good at. What you enjoy doing for fun. How do each of you look different?

There are also unique differences in how each person thinks. Without saying it out loud, think of your favorite animal. On the count of three, everyone say their animal: one, two, three... Did everyone have different answers? Did some of you think of the same animal? Repeat this activity with favorite food, favorite color, favorite toy, etc.

The part of your body that thinks is your brain. God made the human brain so complex, that not even the smartest people understand exactly how it works. God only made one brain like yours. You are fearfully and wonderfully made for His purposes.

Romans 12:2 says, "Do not conform to the pattern of this world, but be transformed by the renewing of your mind. Then you will be able to test and approve what God's will is—His good, pleasing and perfect will."

To be transformed is to be changed by God. We cannot do this alone, no matter how hard we try. This is a change that God does in us. He reshapes our brains as we grow and learn. When our minds are renewed, we learn to think biblically. We learn to honor God in how we act, we have mercy on those in need, and we see sin for what it is.

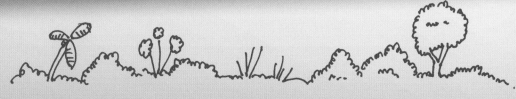

DO NOT CONFORM TO THE PATTERN OF THIS WORLD

ACTIVITY 1

1. Do not let the world push your mind into its pattern, but let God shape your mind from within. Then you can live God's plan, and obey His commands.

2. Place the cards with various locations in the paper bag.

3. Pass the bag to the first student, have him/her pull a card out of the bag. Ask the following questions:

   a. What would someone do in this place who is conformed to the world and does not follow Jesus?

      i. For instance, at a grocery store, someone who does not follow Jesus' commands might cut in line or steal.

   b. What would someone do whose mind is transformed by God?

      i. For instance, at a grocery store, someone who does follow Jesus' teaching might help someone get their groceries to their car or give someone money who did not have enough to pay.

   c. Encourage discussion.

4. Pass the bag to the second student and discuss how to follow Jesus while at that location. Continue passing the bag and discussing what it means to have a mind that is transformed by God until you complete the locations.

 # BRAIN ACTIVITY 2

Glue the brain cut outs onto the photos. Older children can label "brain".

THE NEURON

ACTIVITY 3

1. Have each child draw a neuron the length of a piece of paper.

2. Older children can label:

   dendrites, soma, axon, and terminal buttons.

3. Draw arrows to show the direction of travel of a signal: from the dendrites, down the axon, off the terminal buttons. Explain that all of the neurons line up and send messages only one way. There are other neurons that line up to send signals the other direction. Like two one way streets; cars go east on one street and west on the other street.

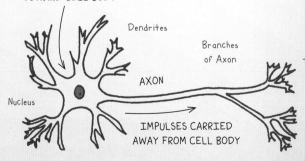

IMPULSES CARRIED TOWARD CELL BODY

Dendrites

Branches of Axon

Termin button

AXON

Nucleus

IMPULSES CARRIED AWAY FROM CELL BODY

Soma

NEURAL CONDUCTION

1. Ask everyone to wiggle their toes (remove shoes if appropriate).

2. Let's study how that message was sent (have a child stand up to use as an example; the other children should follow along on their bodies):

    a. Touch the child's ear. First, the ear heard, the teacher say, "wiggle your toes."

    b. Touch the child's head. That message went from your ear, to your brain. The brain considered the instructions.

    c. Run your finger down the child's spine. Then, the brain sent the message down, down, down the spinal cord. The spinal cord attaches your brain to the rest of your body. Say "spinal cord" several times.

    d. Run your finger down the child's leg. Then, the message was sent to a peripheral nerve that runs down your leg all the way to your toes.

    e. Point to the child's toes. And the toe muscles received the message and moved your toes up and down.

    f. This whole process is possible because the message is passed along from one neuron to the next.

3. Review this series of events a few times if needed. It is also interesting to consider how fast neural conduction occurs. It is almost instantaneous. But explaining it takes several minutes.

4. Neurons also allow us to feel all kinds of things. Blindfold one child. Ask, "where am I touching you?" Put pressure on his/her knee, arm, hand, etc. How do you know where I am touching you?

    a. The neurons in your knee send the message

    b. up the peripheral nerve in your leg

    c. to the spinal cord

    d. which sends the message to your brain

    e. which thinks "knee!"

    f. which sends a message to your vocal chords and mouth to say, "knee!"

5. Ask for volunteers to wear the blindfold and volunteers to trace the neural pathway from an extremity to the brain.

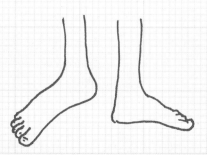

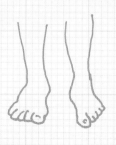
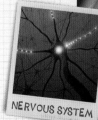

NERVOUS SYSTEM

SENDING A MESSAGE

ACTIVITY 5

[Requires at least one adult and two children]

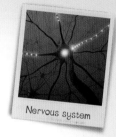

Nervous system

1. Tape the neurons created in activity 2 to each child's chest. All neurons need to be pointed the same direction.

2. Line the children up in a row and ask them to hold hands.

3. Explain: In your peripheral nervous system, the neurons are all lined up, ready to send a message. The message only goes one way down the neurons; and it jumps from neuron to neuron. We are going to pretend that we are neurons conducting a message.

4. The adult is the "brain". She holds the hand of the first child on the dendrite end. She thinks of a message and whispers it to the first child (like: "wave your hand" or "kick your foot").

5. The first child does not perform the task, but whispers the message to the second child, who whispers the message to the third child, etc.

6. The last child in the chain does what the message said.

7. Repeat steps 4-6 allowing the children to change positions. Make sure the message always travels from the dendrite end to the terminal button end.

- Every time your child mentions something sensory, ask "how do you know?" For instance, if she says "my feet are wet."

    o The neurons in her feet send the message up the peripheral nerve in her leg,

    o to her spinal cord

    o up to her brain

    o which thinks "wet feet."

    o Her brain then sends the message to her mouth

    o which speaks the words "my feet are wet."

- Study the transformation of Saul / Paul in Acts 9.

    How did Jesus change him?

    How did Paul change his behavior to reflect this change?

APPLY IT

GO BEYOND

Use a paint pen to draw the spinal cord and some peripheral nerves on the child's photo. Label and understand that the brain and spinal cord make up the central nervous system, while the rest of the nerves make up the peripheral nervous system.

MUSCLES

Label the basic muscle groups of the human body. Explore how muscles pull. Consider myocytes and myofibrils of muscle tissue.

BIG IDEA

Who can jump high?
Let me see you jump high.

Can anyone do a push up?

How about a sit up?

What makes you strong?

Who is the strongest person you know?

MATERIALS

1. A long, soft rope for tug-of-war.
2. Rubber bands (preferably red).
3. Small object with flat sides that will not roll (like a dice).
4. 8 x 10 full body photo of each child (to be used throughout the anatomy lessons).
5. Red photo marker or sharpie.
6. Red markers/ crayons, paper.

Muscles are an important part of being strong. God made your bodies full of springy muscle tissue to help you run, dance, talk, digest food, even pump our blood.

Have your muscles ever let you down? Have you ever tripped and fallen? Have you ever dropped something you were carrying? Have you ever spilled your drink at the table?

Psalm 73:26 tells us, "My flesh and my heart may fail, but God is the strength of my heart and my portion forever."

The word "flesh" in this verse is talking about our human bodies, our skin, and our muscles. And the "heart" in this verse is talking about our human courage. Neither our bodies nor our courage is enough to endure in this broken world. We can get sick and hurt. We forget God's commands and make mistakes. The good news is God provides all we lack. When we put our trust in the LORD, we can rely on His strength forever!

You may still trip and fall. You may still get sick. You may still make mistakes, but the LORD will provide you with peace and hope.

MUSCLES

TUG-OF-WAR

1. Divide the children into two groups
   a. One group with all of the older, bigger children
   b. One group with the younger, smaller children
2. Give each group one end of the rope.
   Ask, does this seem like a fair game? Who do you think is going to win?
3. Have them compete in tug-of-war. Warn the older children not to hurt the younger ones.
4. When the older children win, point out that this is how our broken world can defeat us. We are too small and weak to have a chance.
5. Divide the children in the same two groups. But this time have at least one adult join the younger children. Who do you think is going to win this time?
6. Compete in tug-of-war again.
7. When the younger children win, point out that God is our strength. Just as the adult helped the weaker children win the game, so God helps us succeed. He gives us the strength to persevere and succeed at following God, obeying and trusting in him.

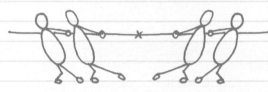

MUSCLES ONLY PULL, NEVER PUSH

1. Now that everyone's muscles have been exercised in that game of tug-of-war, let's learn how exactly you were able to pull.
2. On a clean piece of paper, have each child outline a muscle shape. It should be oblong-shaped (like a football in the U.S.A. or a rugby ball in the rest of the world). You can have a child or adult flex his/her bicep to see the general shape of a muscle.
3. Draw dozens of long red lines inside the outline running from tip to tip. Label these as "myocytes." They are the muscle cells.
4. Explain that inside each myocyte God placed lots of tiny little myofibrils. They are what make us move.
5. Before you give the children their rubber bands and dice, explain the rules:
   a. You may not shoot or pop your neighbor or yourself.
   b. You may touch the rubber band, but not the die (or other small, non-rolling object)
6. Give each child a red rubber band and a die. Ask them to use the rubber band to PUSH the die across the table, without touching the object with their fingers. It will prove difficult, if not impossible.
7. Then have the children loop their rubber bands around the small object and PULL it across the table. This will be much easier. God designed our muscles to be pullers, not pushers. If you push on something, your muscles are using your bones as levers. **Muscles only pull, never push.**
8. Staple the rubber band to each child's muscle picture along the myocytes they drew. Label it as a "myofibril."

MUSCLES

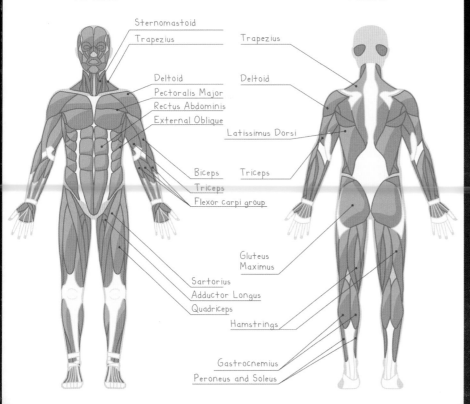

HUMAN MUSCULAR SYSTEM

VENTRAL

DORSAL

Sternomastoid
Trapezius
Trapezius
Deltoid
Deltoid
Pectoralis Major
Rectus Abdominis
External Oblique
Latissimus Dorsi
Biceps
Triceps
Triceps
Flexor carpi group
Gluteus Maximus
Sartorius
Adductor Longus
Quadriceps
Hamstrings
Gastrocnemius
Peroneus and Soleus

MAJOR SKELETAL MUSCLE GROUPS

1. On the 8x10 photo. Ask the children to draw the following muscle groups. Red sharpies or paint pens work best on photo paper.

    a. Remind them of the shape of a muscle.

    b. Guide them to draw the muscles so they go approximately from joint to joint.

    c. Bicep, tricep, deltoid, pectoralis, abdominals, quadricep, gastrocnemius. (There are about 640 muscles in the human body. So feel free to extend this list).

2. Older children can label the muscles. You can create labels for younger children to glue down.

VOLUNTARY VERSUS INVOLUNTARY

1. Have you ever heard someone say, "I need a volunteer"? What are they asking for? Someone to willingly do a job or help out.

2. You have muscles that are willing to do a job and help out too. They are called your voluntary muscles. Your voluntary muscles are the ones you control. When you "ask" them to move, your brain sends the message to contract or relax. And the muscles obey by running, walking, riding, waving, and moving your bones all around. All of the muscles from Activity 3 are voluntary muscles.

3. The other class of muscles are called involuntary muscles. This does not mean they are not willing to do a job and help out. It simply means that you do not have control over them. Your body works hard all of the time without you even thinking about it. Have you ever had to tell your heart to beat? No. That is because you heart is an involuntary muscle. Have you ever had goose bumps? The tiny muscles that attach to the hairs on your arm make them stand up when

you are cold. Have you ever had to tell your stomach to digest breakfast? Your digestive track is made of involuntary muscles that digest food without you even thinking about it. Involuntary muscles work day and night, and you don't ever have to boss them around or tell them to "get back to work." Didn't God give you an amazing body!

4. Play "Simon Says." The teacher can say "Simon says to use your hamstrings" or "Simon says flex your biceps." These use voluntary skeletal muscles. The teacher can also use commands for involuntary muscles, like "Simon says for your heart to beat." In which case the children should say "Involuntary!". Some involuntary muscles you might use are contract the pupils of your eyes or use your small intestine to digest food. Breathing is tricky because you do have some control over it, but the respiratory tract is made of involuntary muscles. Then have students act as Simon and call out instructions.

- When your child is playing, ask which muscles she is using. For instance biceps and quadriceps for pumping a swing, quadriceps for running, pectorals for steering a bike.

- When you buy a piece of unground beef, ask your child to point out the myocytes/ muscle fibers.

- Study the story of David and Goliath from 1 Samuel 17.

    o Who was stronger, David or Goliath?

    o How did David win?

    o Did David have faith that God would help him? How do you know David had faith?

    o Are you facing any "giants" in your life? How might God help you overcome those problems?

    o How can you have faith like David?

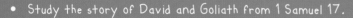

GO BEYOND

- While wearing swimming suits, use a washable marker or face paint crayons, write the basic muscle groups on your child's body. And allow your child to write the basic muscle groups on a parent's body.

- Explore the differences in voluntary and involuntary muscle contraction.

    • Examine a thin slice of raw beef roast or steak under a microscope. Can you see the myocytes?

Blood vessels and nerves

One fascicle (bundle of muscle fibers)

Myocyte

Muscle

Connective tissue

Myofibril

MUSCLES

BONES

Identify and label the major bones of the body. Understand that bones give your body structure. Create a song to learn the bones.

MATERIALS

1. A large bed sheet.
2. A few pillows.
3. At least two chairs.
4. 8 x 10 photo of each child.
5. A big paper skeleton or model plastic skeleton.

Give the children the sheet and the pillows. Ask them to build a fort, using only the sheet and pillows. Let them work until they are slightly frustrated. What does this fort need? Would some chairs help? Give the children the chairs so they can rebuild the fort. Help them build it big and strong.

BIG IDEA

Nehemiah 8:10 tell us that "The joy of the LORD is your strength."

If we do not have the joy of the LORD in our hearts, our lives will be a big mess. Like the fort you built with only a sheet and pillows. Did it stand up? Was it a good fort? We cannot stand upon the promises of this world; they will fail, and we will fall. But the joy of the LORD is amazingly powerful. If you have the joy of the LORD in your heart, He will be your strength. Like the fort with the chairs stood strong.

If your body had only skin and muscles, you would look like the first fort. Your body would be a pile on the floor. But God gave our bodies something to help us stand up. Do you know what helps your body stand up? Bones!

What are bones? What did God make them to do? Where are your bones?

What would your body be like without bones?

Your bones give your body structure.

Did you know that there are 206 bones in the human body? We are going to learn just a few.

ACTIVITY 1

BONES SONG

Make up a song to the tune of "Dem Bones" to playfully sing the correct names of all of the bones while the children dance and point to their bones.

BONES

MAJOR BONES

ACTIVITY 2

1. On the 8 x 10 photo. It is very difficult to draw or glue bones on the photos because so many of the bones overlap or are so small. Children can label the bones on the appropriate limb with the understanding that the bone supports the limb. You can create labels for younger children to glue down on the appropriate limb.

2. Beginning at the top, label the locations of the following bones:

   a. Cranium, mandible

   b. Clavicle, scapula, humerus, radius, ulna, carpals, metacarpals, phalanges

   c. Vertebrae, ribs, sternum

   d. Pelvis, femur, patella, tibia, fibula, tarsals, metatarsals, phalanges

3. Note that in the lists above, list "a" and list "c" make up the axial skeleton. List "b" and list "d" make up the appendicular skeleton.

Skeleton diagram labels: Cranium, Mandible, Cervical Vertebrae, Thoracic vertebrae, Lumbar vertebrae, Pelvis, Sacrum, Coccyx, Tarsals, Metatarsals, Phalanges, Clavicle, Scapula, Sternum, Ribs, Humerus, Radius, Ulna, Carpals, Metacarpals, Phalanges, Femur, Patella, Tibia, Fibula, Calcaneus

BONES GAME

ACTIVITY 3

1. Create labels from note cards or card stock of each of the learned bones. The teacher can do this before hand or have the students create the labels.

2. Place painter's tape on each label.

3. Without the students watching, hide the labels around the classroom, house, or playground.

4. Then, ask students to find ONE label at a time.

5. When one label is found, the student may attempt to place the label on the correct bone of the model skeleton.

6. If the student correctly places the label, write his initials on the label.

7. If he misplaces the label, tell him to go re-hide it and return with one different label.

8. Continue until all labels are found and correctly placed.

APPLY IT

- When your child gets hurt, refer to the bone. For instance, instead of saying, "I'm so sorry you banged your knee" say "I'm so sorry you banged your patella."

- Share a glass of milk with your child. Discuss the importance of calcium in the human body. It is important for strong bones and teeth. Most calcium is stored in bones and teeth (Osteoblasts are the cells that build bone). And there is also a little calcium in the blood. People need to eat plenty of dairy products, leafy greens, and dried beans.

  If they don't, their bodies will pull calcium OUT of the bones to replace the calcium in the blood (Osteoclasts are the cells that break bone down). What do you think happens to the bones of a person who does not get enough calcium?

- Learn to identify more of the 206 bones in the adult human body.

- Allowing your children to examine how their own joints move.
  Can they find an example of each of the following synovial joints?

  o Ball and Socket – allow a limb to move in many different directions (hip and shoulder)

  o Hinge – back and forth like the opening and closing of a door (elbow and knee)

  o Ellipsoidal – allow rocking from side to side, but limited rotation (base of index finger)

  o Pivot – turn side to side (neck)

GO BEYOND

Other types of joints:

  o Fixed joints – bones connected by fibrous tissue, no movement (skull)

  o Slightly movable joints – bones connected by cartilage pads, only small movements (spine)

ACTIVITY

FUNCTION OF BONES

Understand the structure and functions of a mammalian long bone.

MATERIALS

1. Crayons or colored pencils.

2. A cut away example bone (from a roast, rib, or pork chop).

For an extra activity on bones visit this book's page on the website christianfocus.com

WHAT IS INSIDE A BONE?

1. Why did God give us bones? (to help us stand up and move). But God placed a secret inside your bones. They actually make – BLOOD!

2. While you construct the following diagram of a bone, study the example bone you brought.

3. Give each child a piece of paper and crayons. Ask them to draw a big bone shape.

4. Draw a second line around the whole entire bone. Then lightly cross hatch and/or scribble inside the inner line.

   a. The outside of the bone is covered with a thin, touch membrane called the periosteum. Blood vessels and nerves enter and exit the bone through the periosteum.

      i. Label the outside line of the bone as the periosteum.

      ii. The periosteum is somewhat fragile, so it may be missing from your example bone.

   b. Below the periosteum is hard, dense compact bone.

However, it is not completely solid. Small holes for nerves and blood vessels run through the compact bone. Compact bone gives your bones strength.

      i. Label the space between the two lines as compact bone.

      ii. Can you find the compact bone on the example bone?

   c. The inside of the bone is spongy bone. It is full of small spaces containing bone marrow. Red bone marrow is found through the length of the bone. It is responsible for producing red blood cells. Yellow bone marrow is found at the ends of the bone. It is responsible for storing fat.

      i. Color the length of the inside of the bone red and label it as red bone marrow.

      ii. Color the ends of the inside of the bone yellow and label them as yellow bone marrow.

      iii. Can you find the bone marrow on the example bone?

BONES

Experiment 18:

RESPIRATORY SYSTEM

Identify and label the trachea and lungs.
Explore how myocytes use oxygen and create carbon dioxide, red blood cells carry gasses, and alveoli perform gas exchange in the lungs.

MATERIALS

1. A single die.

2. Small box so the die can be rolled secretly.

3. 8 x 10 photo of each child.

4. Before the lesson cut out two pink oval shaped paper lungs for each child's photo.

5. Red photo marker or sharpie.

5. Signs to tape on each child's chest:
   alveolus, red blood cell, myocyte,

6. Tinker toys or blocks to build 5-10 representations of both O=O (oxygen gas) and O=C=O (carbon dioxide).

   Alternatively, a molecular model kit, Styrofoam balls, or marshmallows with sticks can be used to construct the gas molecules.

BIG IDEA

Everyone take a deep breath in... and back out... and back in... and back out. New rule: for the rest of the lesson, NO MORE BREATHING! (Pause for a moment.) Why are you breaking the rule?

God created your bodies so that you breathe all the time. What can you do to make your body breathe faster? What about running in place? Or jumping? What about when you are sleeping, do you breathe quickly or slowly?

Can you talk without breathing? You have to breathe for air to pass over your vocal cords. This is how you talk and sing.

Psalm 150:6 Says "Let everything that has breath praise the LORD. Praise the LORD!"

RESPIRATORY SYSTEM

What is something you give praise for? God is all powerful and all knowing. He is the creator of the universe and everything in it. Praise is an important way we can surrender to God. You can sing praise, shout praise, whisper praise, or say praise. God does not care how you praise him. Take turns giving the LORD praise. Say a prayer of praise before starting the lesson.

The Bible tells about many people who praise God, but one man named David really enjoyed praising God.

Read one of David's songs of praise in Psalm 145. Read it a second time and ask the children to say "praise" every time they hear David extol God.

PRAISE THE LORD

1. If you are breathing, you have the honor of praising God. Let's make good use of our breath.

2. Let one student roll the die in the box.

3. The student is not to say the number out loud, but clap the number on the die.

4. The other students listen to how many claps, then take a big deep breath, and all shout, "Praise the Lord!" to equal the number of claps.

5. It takes breath to shout praise to the LORD. Today, we are going to learn how God created your body to breathe.

LUNGS AND TRACHEA

ACTIVITY 2

1. Use glue sticks to attach two lungs to the chest area of each child's photo.

an upside down "Y" connecting the throat to the two lungs

2. Then have them draw a trachea, which is like

3. Older children can label lungs and trachea.

ACT OUT RESPIRATION

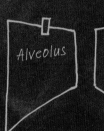 

Alveolus   Myocyte

ACTIVITY 3

(Three people required for this game. If there are more people, it is great to have multiple alveoli, red blood cells, and myocytes).

1. If you have not done so already, build 5–10 representations of both O=O (oxygen gas) and O=C=O (carbon dioxide).

2. On one side of the room, label a person as an alveolus in a lung– this is the site of gas exchange.

   a. The alveolus does not move from this place. It stays in the lung.

   b. The job of the alveolus is to pick up oxygen molecules from the "air" and transfer them to the red blood cell.

   c. They are also to take the carbon dioxide molecule from the red blood cell and release it back to the air.

   d. The alveolus starts the game with a pile of oxygen molecules ready to be exchanged.

3. On the opposite side of the room, the second person is a myocyte (muscle cell) in a quadricep. The myocyte does not move from this place; it stays in the muscle.

   a. The myocyte person is to run in place. The job of the myocyte is to exercise, which causes it to use oxygen and make carbon dioxide.

   b. So the myocyte will take the oxygen molecules from the red blood cell and give carbon dioxide to the red blood cell.

   c. The myocyte starts the game with a pile of carbon dioxide molecules ready to be exchanged.

Act Out Respiration (Continued)

4. The third person is a red blood cell. This student is going to run back and forth between the alveolus and the myocyte.

   a. The job of the red blood cell is to deliver oxygen from the alveolus to the entire body through the circulatory system.

   b. In this game the myocyte will need the oxygen. The red blood cell is also going to take oxygen from the alveolus and take it to the myocyte, then return carbon dioxide from the myocyte to the alveolus. (In reality, however, most waste carbon dioxide is transported back to the lungs as bicarbonate (HCO_3-) dissolved in blood plasma).

   c. The red blood cell starts the game standing by the alveolus, ready to accept the oxygen molecule and run to deliver it to the myocyte.

5. On your mark... get set... respirate!

6. The alveolus hands an oxygen molecule to the red blood cell (breathe in).

7. The red blood cell walks quickly to the myocyte (which is exercising in place) and exchanges the oxygen molecule for a carbon dioxide molecule.

8. The red blood cell carries the carbon dioxide back to the alveoli, hands the carbon dioxide to the alveoli (breathe out), and picks up another oxygen (breathe in).

9. Repeat steps 6–8 until all of the oxygen and carbon dioxide are used up (all of the oxygen are at the myocyte and all of the carbon dioxide are at the alveolus).

10. Everyone exchange roles and repeat the activity.

| LUNG | <---> | BLOOD STREAM | <---> | MUSCLE |

| Alveolus (with oxygen) | <----> | Red blood cell | <----> | Myocyte (with carbon dioxide) |

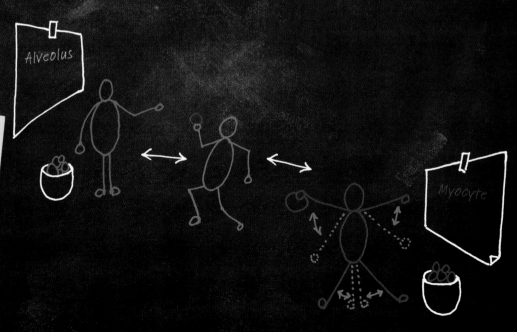

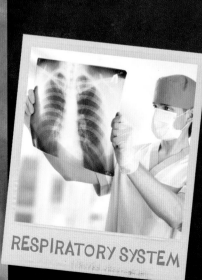

RESPIRATORY SYSTEM

APPLY IT

- Whenever you notice your child breathing hard from exercise, ask: Why are you breathing so hard? What is happening in your body? What are your alveoli doing? What are your red blood cells doing? What are your myocytes doing?

- How can you praise the LORD with your breath? Practice singing, shouting, praying, giving thanks to God for all He has done. Read Psalm 138, Psalm 103, and 2 Samuel 22. How does David praise God?

What do these two Psalms say about other ways to praise God?
Psalm 149:3 and Psalm 134:2.

STRUCTURE & FUNCTION OF THE DIAPHRAGM.

ACTIVITY

1. Tie the neck of one balloon. Cut the big end off (without the knot) and discard. Keep the piece of balloon with the knot.
2. Cut off the bottom of the bottle. Stretch the tied end of the balloon around the open bottom of the bottle. Tape it in place.
3. Slip the straw into the neck of the other balloon and secure it with tape so air cannot get around the balloon.
4. Place the straw and the balloon into the top of the bottle and seal the neck of the bottle with clay or playdough.
5. This is a model lung:
   1. The straw is the trachea
   2. The balloon is the lung
   3. The bottle is the chest cavity/rib cage
   4. The bottom balloon is the diaphragm.
6. Hold the bottle and gently pull the knot on the bottom balloon. What happens to the inner balloon? When we breathe in, the diaphragm at the bottom of the chest cavity pulls down, creating space in the lungs. Air is then taken in through the mouth and nose, down the trachea, to the lungs. When we breathe out, the diaphragm rises, pushing air out of the lungs, up the trachea, out the nose and mouth.

MATERIALS

1. Small plastic soda bottle.
2. Straw.
3. Scissors.
4. 2 medium/large latex balloons.
5. Tape.
6. Clay or playdough.

Photosynthesis — Oxygen — Respiration — Carbon Dioxide

God made a wonderful balance between plants and animals. He created plants to use carbon dioxide and create oxygen through photosynthesis, while animals and people use oxygen and create carbon dioxide through respiration. Go outside among some trees and discuss this process. Have your child draw a picture of himself beside a tree. Use arrows to show the oxygen and carbon dioxide trade off.

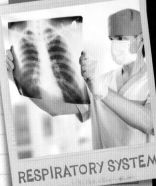

RESPIRATORY SYSTEM

CIRCULATORY SYSTEM

Understand the structure and function of the heart, arteries, and veins.
Explore the four basic ingredients in human blood.

MATERIALS

1. A shaker of ground black pepper.
2. Liquid dish soap.
3. A toothpick.
4. A very clean oil free white or glass mixing bowl half full of water.
5. 8 x 10 photo of each child.
6. Before the lesson cut out one small red paper heart for each child's photo.
7. Model oxygen gas molecule and model carbon dioxide gas molecule (as used in the respiratory system lesson).
8. Six simple costumes:
   - Soldier or Knight (white blood cell) = toy sword and/or shield.
   - Food server (plasma) = toy food and/or tea set.
   - Fix-it-man (platelets) = toy tools, hammer, wrench, etc.
   - Fast flying fairy (red blood cell) = butterfly or fairy wings.
   - Germ = Scary costume, mask, or label.
   - Myocyte = Red shirt or label.

(If you have more than six students, create multiples of the costumes. If you have less than six students, adults can be the germ and myocyte, and the child(ren) can be each of the other components in turn).

Where are the muscles in your body? Allow children to show their muscles.

Did you know there are muscles in your body that you don't even have to control or think about? There is one very important muscle that words all the time to pump blood through your whole body. What is it? Your heart! The red oxygenated blood is pumped away from your lungs and heart through arteries (remember "arteries away"). Then it gives nourishment and oxygen to the cells in your toes, brain, fingers, liver, etc. Then the blood travels back to your heart through veins (remember "veins reverse"). The blood has much less oxygen, so it is a darker color. This causes veins to appear blue through your skin (note: the blood is not blue, but a darker red. It is a combination of light refraction and skin tone that causes veins to appear blue). Can you see the blue veins in your wrist? Can you see blue veins in the eye lids of your friend?

BIG IDEA

God made your body so the arteries are deep in your body, protected by muscles and skin, like in your arms and legs. This is in case you are injured there is less chance of an artery getting bruised or cut. So you can't see your arteries, but you can feel them. You can feel your artery walls stretch and relax with every beat of your heart. Can anyone find their pulse? Can you feel your pulse on the carotid artery in your neck? Can you feel your pulse on the radial artery in your wrist?

Arteries and veins are both types of blood vessels.

CIRCULATORY SYSTEM

What makes your heart beat faster?

Can you run in place and feel your pulse speed up?

Exercise is a great reason for your heart to beat fast. It is healthy and good for your heart. But have you ever felt your heart race when you were scared, worried, or startled? The Bible tells us what to do in this situation.

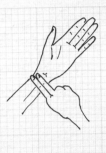

CIRCULATORY SYSTEM

In Philippians 4:6-7 Paul says, "Do not be anxious about anything, but in every situation, by prayer and petition, with thanksgiving, present your requests to God. And the peace of God, which transcends all understanding, will guard your hearts and your minds in Christ Jesus."

THE PEACE OF GOD

ACTIVITY 1

1. Have the children sit in a circle around the mixing bowl of water. The mixing bowl of water is your "heart and mind." Please instruct children not to touch the water too much as the oil from their hands can mess up the experiment.

2. Hand one child the pepper shaker and ask, "What worries you? What are you scared about? What are you anxious about? What makes your heart beat fast?" For each worry he mentions, ask him to shake the pepper once into the bowl.

3. Go around the circle encouraging children to share their fears and worries and shake pepper onto the surface of the water. Try not to bump the bowl, this may break the surface tension of the water and cause the pepper to sink. The water will be covered in black flecks. These represent our worries and fears clouding our heart and mind.

4. Form a hypothesis: what will happen if I put a drop of soap in the bowl? Allow children to brainstorm.

5. Place one drop of liquid dish soap on the table. Dip the toothpick in it, then touch it to the water in the middle of the bowl. What happens to the pepper? The soap is "peace of God." It clears your heart and mind of all of the worries.

6. Read Philippians 4:6 very carefully, outlining the steps to a prayer for peace:

   - In EVERY situation
   - By prayer and petition (asking)
   - With thanksgiving
   - Present your request to God

7. Pray with the children following these steps from Philippians 4:6.

8. Why does the pepper run from the soap? Soap breaks down the surface tension of the water. Surface tension is what holds water molecules together, like they are holding hands. The soap breaks the surface tension, so some of the pepper falls through the water because it can no longer float on top. The water molecules would like to maintain that surface tension as much as possible, so they pull back away from the soap and carry the pepper along with them.

ACT OUT THE PARTS OF THE BLOOD

(the more people you have for this game, the better)

God created your body to do so many things. Has anyone ever skinned their knee? Or cut their finger? What about a bruise? Did your body heal? Have you ever had a cold? Did you get well? God created your blood full of tiny cells and special ingredients that work hard to keep you healthy. We are going to act out the parts of the blood that keep you going.

1. Dress one student as a soldier, the white blood cell. Ready to fight any germs that might attack.

   a. White blood cells are part of your immune system; they defend the body against any germs that want to make it sick. Has anyone ever had a bad cold? White blood cells helped you get well by "killing" the cold virus.

2. Dress one student as a food server, the plasma. He will carry food to the "hungry" myocyte.

   a. Plasma transports nutrients from the digestive system to cells. When you eat breakfast, the nutrients are broken down into tiny molecules by your digestive system, then your blood plasma carries the nutrients to the cells in your brain, legs, fingers, etc. Plasma is not cells, it is mostly water. Besides transporting nutrients, plasma also carries the other parts of the blood along.

3. Dress one student as the fix-it-man, platelets. He will fix any cuts he finds.

   a. Platelets form clots and scabs when you have a scrape or bruise. They fix bleeding and broken vesicles. Does anyone have a scab? This is made possible by your platelets!

4. Dress one student as the fast flying fairy, a red blood cell. She will carry oxygen to the myocyte and pick up carbon dioxide from the myocyte.

   a. Red Blood cells carry oxygen so your cells can keep working (cellular respiration). The harder your body works, the more oxygen your muscle cells (myocytes) need. So your heart pumps your blood faster so more oxygen can be delivered to your cells by the red blood cells.

5. One person acts as a scary "germ" for the white blood cell to attack.

6. Another person acts like a hungry myocyte, carrying too much CO_2 and in need of oxygen from the red blood cell and nutrients from the plasma. The myocyte stands still and does not move with the blood.

7. A long hallway works best for this next part; it simulates a blood vessel. Make sure all of the doors are open, these are the wounds for the platelet to fix as he closes the doors. In order to represent bruises, turn over a few chairs for the platelet to upright as he passes.

8. Everyone begin at one end of the hallway; stay together and travel down the hallway searching for opportunities to perform the functions of the various parts of the blood. Explain the path of blood as you go: Starting at the heart, the blood travels a short distance to the alveoli of the lungs where it exchanges carbon dioxide for oxygen, then it travels back to the heart, and finally is pumped out the aorta and through arteries to all the parts of the body.

   a. White blood cell fights the germ

   b. Plasma carries food to the myocyte and makes sure everyone stays together

   c. Platelet closes all of the doors and uprights the chairs to stop bleeding

   d. Red blood cell carries oxygen molecule to the myocyte and takes the carbon dioxide to return.

   e. Blood returns to the heart through veins.

9. Have the students change roles and go down the hallway again. Make sure each child has a turn to be each part of the blood.

CIRCULATORY SYSTEM

HEART

1. Use glue sticks to attach the heart between the lungs of each child's photo.

- Study the pathway of blood through the heart: blood enters the right atrium of the heart, then it goes through the tricuspid valve to the right ventricle, then through the semilunar valves to the pulmonary trunk, then through the pulmonary arteries to the lungs where it is oxygenated, then back to the heart through the pulmonary veins, into the left atrium, through the bicuspid (mitral) valve, into the left ventricle, through the aortic semilunar valves into the aorta, and then distributed to the rest of the body through arteries.

- Explore what makes blood red:
  o Red blood cells contain a protein called hemoglobin. Hemoglobin is made up of smaller units called hemes. The hemes bind with iron molecules, and the iron molecules are actually what bind with oxygen. The red color is because of the iron/oxygen interaction, similar to what makes iron rust orange.

BLOOD DROP

MATERIALS

1. Crayons or markers.
2. One piece of paper for each child.
3. Several copies or sketches of the blood components pictured to the right.

ACTIVITY

1. Cut out the white blood cells, platelets, and red blood cells ahead of time for smaller children. Older children can cut them out themselves.

2. Have each child draw a large drop shape to fill his/her paper.

3. Ask children to glue down the white blood cell on the blood drop. As they glue remind them of the function of the white blood cells. Ask them to decorate their white blood cell with weapons to defend the body against germs.

4. Ask the children to glue down the platelet on the blood drop. As they glue, remind them of the function of the platelets. Ask them to decorate their platelet with tools for fixing cuts and bruises.

5. Ask the children to glue down the red blood cell. Remind them of the function of the red blood cells. Have them write O_2 on their red blood cell and color it red.

6. Color the remainder of the blood drop yellow. This is the plasma. Remind them that plasma transports nutrients. Ask them to draw their favorite foods in the yellow plasma.

White Blood Cell

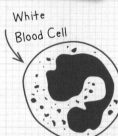

Platelet

Red Blood Cell

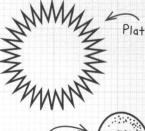

DIGESTIVE SYSTEM

Understand the path of food through the digestive system.

MATERIALS

1. 8 x 10 photo of each child.
2. Before the lesson cut out a red kidney shaped stomach and a brown triangle-shaped liver for each child.
3. Red, brown, orange, and green photo marker or sharpie.
4. A long leg of a pair of panty hose or tights with the toe cut out.
5. Several balls of a size to squeeze through the leg of the panty hose, but not fall straight through.

DIGESTIVE SYSTEM

BIG IDEA

When Jesus came to earth, he was all human and all God. And just as humans do, he felt cheerful, sad, tired, happy, excited, angry, and sometimes even hungry. Here is a story from Matthew 4:1–11 a time when Jesus was really hungry.

One day, Jesus went to the desert. He went there to be away from people and distractions. He wanted to pray and spend time with God, His Father. Jesus fasted while he was in the desert. He did not eat anything for forty days!

Do you think he was hungry?

Then, the devil came to try to talk Jesus into doing something wrong. First, the devil said, "If you are the Son of God, tell these stones to become bread." Does that sound like a good idea? Jesus was hungry, but He knew it was always wrong to listen to the devil. So He said a verse from the Scriptures:

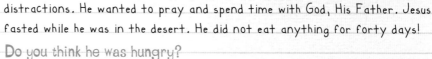

In Matthew 4:4, Jesus said, "It is written: 'Man shall not live on bread alone, but on every word that comes from the mouth of God.'"

The devil did not leave Jesus alone. He took Jesus to the top of the Temple in Jerusalem. He told Jesus, "If you are the Son of God, "he said, "throw yourself down. For it is written:

"'He will command his angels concerning you, and they will lift you up in their hands, so that you will not strike your foot against a stone.'"

Again, Jesus quoted Scripture, "It is also written: 'Do not put the LORD your God to the test.'"

Then, the devil took Jesus up on a high mountain. He told Jesus He could rule over all the countries in the world. All Jesus would have to do is bow down and worship the devil. Jesus rebuked the devil and said, "Away from me, Satan! For it is written: 'Worship the LORD your God, and serve him only.'"

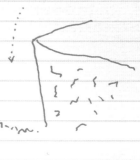

Finally, the devil left and angels came to take care of Jesus. Satan tried to tempt Jesus, but Jesus would not do anything wrong. He did not sin.

Discuss the following points of this story:

- Jesus was hungry and alone when Satan came to him. We need to be most careful of temptation when we are weak or tired. This is when we are most likely to make mistakes.

- Satan did not give up after one try. He did not go away until Jesus commanded him. When temptation comes our way, be aware that there may be multiple temptations at the same time.

DIGESTIVE SYSTEM

- Jesus had already decided that He would not sin. Jesus did not wait until the devil was talking about bread to choose whether or not He would listen to the devil. We need to make up our minds to follow Jesus before temptation comes our way.

- Jesus used Scriptures to rebuke Satan. It is important for us to learn our memory verses so we can use them when we are tempted.

THE "WHAT IF" GAME

 ACTIVITY 1

Present the following temptations to the children. Encourage discussion. Use the Scriptures listed to encourage the children.

1. What if you find something that belongs to someone else?
   - Exodus 20:15 says, "You shall not steal."

2. What if you promise your mom that you will read the Bible with her, but a friend asks you to go play?
   - Ephesians 6:1 says, "Children, obey your parents in the LORD, for this is right."

3. What if you know that you will get into trouble if you tell the truth?
   - Proverbs 12:22 says, "The Lord detests lying lips, but he delights in people who are trustworthy."

4. What if friends make fun of you because you will not look at a bad picture on one of their phones?
   - Matthew 6:22 tells us, "The eye is the lamp of the body. If your eyes are healthy, your whole body will be full of light."

PERISTALSIS

 ACTIVITY 2

1. It is a really long way down the entire digestive system, from the mouth, down the esophagus, through the stomach, along the small intestine, through the large intestine, and finally out into the toilet. How does the food move?

2. Hold up the panty hose. This represents the digestive system.

3. Hold up a ball. This represents a bite of food.

4. Place the ball in one end of the panty hose. How can we get this ball to come out the other end?

5. Allow the children to experiment until they figure out that they can squeeze the panty hose directly above the ball in order to propel it downward.

6. Each time they squeeze, say "PERISTALSIS"

7. Peristalsis is the wave like contraction of smooth muscle tissue to propel food through the entire digestive tract.

Structure & Function of the Digestive System

Do you remember how hungry Jesus was in the desert? Have you ever been very hungry? Why does your body need food? Where does your food go when you swallow it?

God designed your body to eat and use all kinds of food. This is <u>digestion</u>; food is broken down to be absorbed by your body. Food gives you energy and keeps you healthy. God designed an amazing pathway called the <u>digestive system</u> that allows your body to get all of the possible nutrients from the food.

Today, we are going to talk about how our bodies digest food. But remember, we need more than food to live for Jesus. The Word of God nourishes your spirit like food nourishes your body.

1. Use a brown sharpie to draw in an <u>esophagus</u> from the mouth down to the abdomen of the child's photo.
   a. Explain: Digestion begins when food enters your mouth. Your <u>saliva</u> is full of enzymes that break down food, and your teeth chew up the food.
   b. Then the food is swallowed down your esophagus to your stomach.

2. Use glue sticks to attach the <u>stomach</u> just to the right of center on the abdomen of the child's photo.
   a. Explain that the purpose of the stomach is to further digest the food with strong acid and enzymes.
   b. The stomach also mixes the food with the enzymes and acid.

3. Use a red sharpie to draw squiggle lines for the <u>small intestine</u> under the stomach.
   a. Explain that the small intestine is a long thin tube; about twenty-three feet long!
   b. The small intestine continues to digest the food while it also absorbs nutrients from the food.
   c. There are three additional organs that help the small intestine continue to digest food.
      i. The <u>pancreas</u> makes a complex mixture of enzymes to help digest fats, carbohydrates, and proteins.
      ii. The <u>liver</u> makes bile to help absorb fats into the bloodstream.
      iii. The <u>gallbladder</u> stores the bile made by the liver until it is needed.

4. Use glue sticks to attach the liver just to the left of center on the abdomen of the child's photo. Draw a small green circle on the liver, near the bottom of the triangle to represent the gallbladder. Draw an orange oval between the stomach and liver to represent the pancreas.

5. Use a brown sharpie to draw an upside down squiggle "U" shape across the abdomen for the <u>large intestine</u> or <u>colon</u>.
   a. Explain that the large intestine is a thick short tube; about five feet long.
   b. The large intestine absorbs water from the remaining indigestible food and then pushes the indigestible food out of the body as feces.

6. Older children can label esophagus, stomach, small intestine, liver, pancreas, gallbladder, and large intestine.

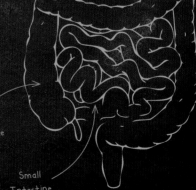

Large Intestine

Small Intestine

DIGESTIVE SYSTEM

APPLY IT

- When sitting down at meal time, trace the path of food through the digestive system, reviewing the function of each part. Remember the hand under hand motion of peristalsis.

- Whenever bread is served at a meal, use it as a reminder to practice Matthew 4:4.

Ask your child if she has ever choked on food or drink?

Ask if she can swallow and breathe at the same time. The epiglottis is a flap of skin that covers the trachea and directs food down the esophagus when swallowing occurs. Add an epiglottis to the throat of the 8 x 10 photo of your child.

GO BEYOND

Observe the movement of an earthworm. They move by a mechanism very similar to peristalsis.

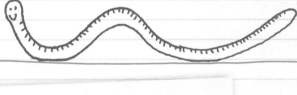

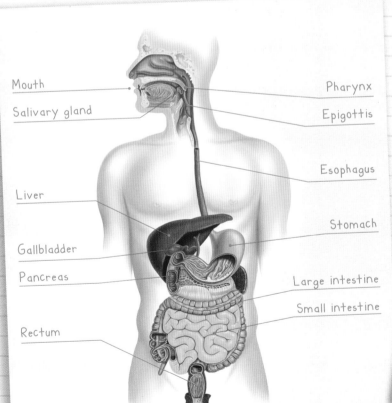

Mouth
Salivary gland
Liver
Gallbladder
Pancreas
Rectum

Pharynx
Epigottis
Esophagus
Stomach
Large intestine
Small intestine

DIGESTIVE SYSTEM

URINARY SYSTEM

Learn the parts of the urinary system. Understand the basic structure and function of the kidneys and bladder. Explore urine's components and how it is produced.

MATERIALS

1. 8 x 10 photo of each child.

2. Before the lesson cut out two small pink kidneys and one yellow bladder for each child's photo.

3. A paint pen or permanent marker.

4. Driver's license size cards labeled: *white blood cell, red blood cell, plasma, platelet, water, salt* and *urea.*

4. One star shaped card labeled "nephron".

5. A circle of chairs or piece of playground equipment to serve as a pretend jail.

Nephron

What are some ways your body is amazing and wonderful?

(Pretty hair, digest food, run fast, think, heal from wounds, pretty eyes, etc.)

You seem to know a lot about your body. Let's see how much we know about each other. Ask the children to divide into pairs (no groups of three, an extra child can pair with the teacher). Give the students one minute to study the details of each other's appearance. Now ask the children to stand back-to-back, and answer the following questions without peeking at their partner.

BIG IDEA

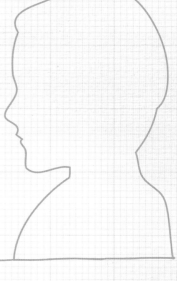

What color is your partner's hair?

What color is your partner's shirt?

What is your partner wearing on his/her feet?

What color are your partner's eyes?

Is your partner wearing a belt?

Is your partner wearing any jewelry?

URINARY SYSTEM

BIG IDEA CONTINUED...

Were these questions easy or hard?

Do you know everything about your partner?

Does anyone know everything about you?

Your parents do not know everything about you. Your friends do not. You don't even know everything about you. But God does. He made you with great care and purpose.

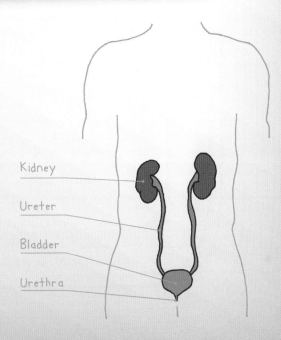

URINARY SYSTEM

Psalm 139:14 "I praise you because I am fearfully and wonderfully made; your works are wonderful, I know that full well."

It's pretty easy to feel special when you know how important you are to God. You were created with great care. We have been studying how God made your body. It is so amazing how God created all of these systems to work together!

Did you know that God even gave you your body filters? Your blood gets "dirty" as it works, so God created an amazing way of getting rid of bad chemicals in your blood. When your liver breaks down proteins, it produces urea. Too much urea in your blood is poisonous. So God made special cells in your kidneys called nephrons to filter the urea out. The nephrons are made to leave the good stuff in your blood, but grab the urea out of your blood. Do you remember the parts of the blood? (The red blood cells, white blood cells, plasma, and platelets). The nephrons let them pass by, but take out the urea. They also remove some salt and some water from the plasma. These three things combine to make urine. The urine then leaves the nephrons in the kidneys and travels down a long tube (ureter) to the bladder. And guess what happens when your bladder is full? You need to go to the bathroom! And the urine travels out of the bladder, down the urethra, into the toilet. God made your kidneys to work all the time, and you don't even have to think about it until it is time to go to the bathroom.

ACTIVITY 1

PARTS OF THE URINARY SYSTEM

1. Use glue sticks to attach two kidneys and a bladder to the lower abdominal area of each child's photo.

2. Then have them draw two ureters from each kidney to the bladder. And a urethra from the bottom of the bladder to the bottom of their body.

3. Older children can label kidneys, ureter, bladder, and urethra.

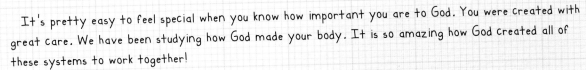

Kidney

Ureter

Bladder

Urethra

ACT OUT URINE COMPONENTS AND NEPHRON FUNCTION

ACTIVITY 2

[More children are better for this game. Alternatively, a group of stuffed animals can substitute for the children].

1. Each child is given a card which will play the part of a "license". Each card has one of the parts of the blood written on it. Make sure each child has one card; it is good to replicate the parts of the blood if more cards are needed.

2. The teacher wears the star-shaped nephron card. In a drill sergeant voice, "I am SERGEANT NEPHRON of the KIDNEY POLICE. And I am here to sort out the parts of the blood. Now get in line!!! Straight and narrow line right down the blood vessel. Have your licenses ready."

I am SERGEANT NEPHRON of the KIDNEY POLICE. And I am here to sort out the parts of the blood. Now get in line!!! Straight and narrow line right down the blood vessel. Have your licenses ready.

3. As the children approach you, carefully read their cards. If they are a good part of the blood (red blood cell, white blood cell, plasma, or platelet) shake their hand and let them circle around to get back in line. Say things like:

   a. "Good job white blood cell. Killed any germs today? Keep up the good work. Continue to circulate."

   b. "Red blood cell, I see you are carrying oxygen. Where are you headed today? Are you going to help a muscle in need? Nice job citizen."

   c. "Find any wounds to heal, platelet? Sorry to hold you up; carry on."

   d. "Oh plasma, you are carrying lots of good food! What was for lunch today? You keep those cells healthy."

4. If the child's card says urea, say, "UREA! No poison allowed in my blood stream!!! TO BLADDER PRISON! Head down the ureter." Send the child to the bladder.

5. If the child's card says water or salt, eye them carefully. Let about half of the water and salt go by and send about half down the ureter to "Bladder Prison."

6. When a few children are in bladder prison, say "This bladder is getting crowded! Down the urethra with all of you!" Pretend "flush" them out of the bladder.

7. Have everyone exchange cards and repeat the activity until attention spans wane.

APPLY IT

- When your child needs to go to the bathroom, review the parts of the urinary system and the components of urine.

- Read Luke 12:7, Psalm 56:8, Ephesians 2:10 and all of Psalm 139. These verses tell us how special we are to God. We should always remember that God made us just the way we are for His purposes and His reasons. Be thankful for the characteristics that make you a unique child of God.

GO BEYOND

- Study kidney transplants. Why they are needed, organ donors, organ recipients, etc.

- Study 1 Corinthians 12. Just as our body systems cooperate, it is important for us to cooperate for God's purposes.

MINI BIOGRAPHIES

GUILLAUME AMONTONS

Guillaume Amontons was born in Paris in 1663, the son of a lawyer. When he was a teenager, he became almost completely deaf. His first attempt at being an inventor was to make a perpetual motion machine. His efforts failed, so he decided to study physics and mathematics. His family strongly opposed this choice, but Amontons pursued his studies.

His first scientific breakthrough was a hygrometer, to measure humidity in the atmosphere. He then developed a shorter barometer, to measure atmospheric pressure. He also worked to create a time-keeping device for ships to solve the problem of knowing longitude. In about 1699, Amontons presented a thermic motor. This machine used hot air and external combustion to create rotation. He then did the first recorded experiments to learn about the friction in machines. Thus, he ascertained the laws of proportionality between friction and the mutual pressure of objects in contact. This led him to make hypothesizes about the causes of earthquakes. He believed there was high pressure air trapped far under the Earth's surface. Amontons continued studying temperature, pressure, and humidity, and was eventually able to develop good alcohol thermometers. Amontons died in Paris in 1705.

("Amontons, Guillaume." Complete Dictionary of Scientific Biography. 2008. Encyclopedia.com. 9 Dec. 2014)

SVANTE ARRHENIUS

Svante Arrhenius was born to a family of farmers in Sweden in 1859. Arrhenius' early education was at a Catholic school, where he showed great aptitude for math and science. When he went to college, Arrhenius studied how various substances conduct electrical current when dissolved in water (electrolytic dissociation). He discovered that neither pure salts nor pure water conduct electricity, but water with salt dissolved in it will conduct electricity. His work was ignored by his professors, but prominent scientists from other universities read his dissertation and came to see him. Later, extensions of this research earned him the Nobel Prize in Chemistry.

He began working for the Academy of Science at Stockholm, doing more research and traveling to consult with other scientists. It was during this period of study that Arrhenius developed the first contemporary definition of acids and bases. He received his Nobel Prize in Chemistry in 1903. His acid-base theory is still widely used. After several years, he began teaching physics at Stockholm's Högskola. The Academy of Sciences in Berlin put Arrhenius in charge of creating a Nobel Institute for Physical Chemistry. He went on to write several science books and often his work was translated into other languages. He wrote on topics such as electrochemistry, the ice age, the greenhouse effect, the aurora borealis, cosmic physics, and smallpox. Arrhenius won many awards for his research and books.

Arrhenius was married twice and had two sons and two daughters. He survived World War I and successfully lobbied for the release of scientists who had been taken prisoners of war. He died in 1927.

("Svante Arrhenius - Biographical". Nobelprize.org. Nobel Media AB 2014. Web. 26 Dec 2014. http://www.nobelprize.org/nobel_prizes/chemistry/laureates/1903/arrhenius-bio.html)

AUGUSTIN DE COULOMB

Charles-Augustin de Coulomb was born in France in 1736 to aristocratic parents. Coulomb went to military school and then to engineering school. His first job was working for the French Government studying the mechanics of dirt. He then worked in architecture, and used calculus to solve problems. This impressed his peers. So he was put in charge of the construction of a wooden fort in Rochefort. While working on the fort, he used the nearby shipyard to do experiments on friction and ropes. From his studies at the shipyard, he wrote an award winning book *Theorie des Machines*

Simples ("Theory of Simple Machines"). Coulomb was then assigned the task of researching and designing a canal. He decided the canal was too expensive, but the French bureaucracy did not believe him. They were rude, so Coulomb quit his job. When an independent study proved that Coulomb was right, the government praised Coulomb for his deduction. But the whole experience upset him so much, from that time on he studied only physics.

He experimented with torsion balance by studying the force of twist on a wire. This research was later used to find the density of planet Earth. But most importantly, Coulomb used torsion balance to measure frictional electricity and magnetism.

During the French Revolution Coulomb retired to a life of studying the friction of pivots, the viscosity of fluids, and how nutrition and environment effect the energy of humans. He was married and had two sons. His name is one of the seventy-two names engraved on the Eiffel Tower. He died in Paris in 1806.

("Charles-Augustin de Coulomb. "Bio. A&E Television Networks, 2014. Web. 12 Dec. 2014.)

BENJAMIN FRANKLIN

Benjamin Franklin was born in Boston, Massachusetts in 1706. He had only two years of formal school because his family could not afford to pay for his education. When he stopped going to school at age 10, his rate of learning actually increased because of his endless curiosity. Franklin was then apprenticed to his older brother in a printing shop. But at age 17, he ran away to Philadelphia to escape the apprenticeship position. At age 23 he began publishing the Philadelphia Gazette. Franklin wrote and published Poor Richard's Almanac, which made him rich. It was a book of forecasts, jokes, stories, and "how to" guides. Franklin continued to self-educate himself, until he was knowledgeable to begin inventing. His inventions include bifocal glasses and the Franklin Stove, which helped people more efficiently heat their homes.

Franklin became fascinated with electricity after seeing a Scottish doctor do demonstrations at a science show. He also proved, famously, that lightening is electricity and invented the lightening rod. His studies of electricity changed the world and formed the language we still use. He coined the terms "positive" and "negative" to describe the direction of flow of electricity. He stated the Law of Conservation of Electric Charge; electrical charge can be collected, but not created. Franklin used the word "battery" to describe his method of collecting electrical charge. In 1751, he published the widely read Experiments and Observations on Electricity. He won the Copley Medal, which was the equivalent of a Nobel Prize. Franklin also studied refrigeration. And upon reaching −14°C (7°F), he said, "One may see the possibility of freezing a man to death on a warm summer's day."

Benjamin Franklin was much more than a scientist and an inventor. He was a husband and a father of two children. He was the postmaster for the colonies, the Ambassador to France, one of the five men who drafted the Declaration of Independence, and the governor of Pennsylvania. He died in 1790.

("Benjamin Franklin." Famous Scientists. famousscientists.org. 1 Jul. 2014. Web. 12/16/2014)

GALILEO GALILEI

Galileo Galilei was born in Pisa, Italy in 1564. He was the first of six children. His father was a musician. In his youth, he was well-educated and smart. He began to study medicine, and then changed to mathematics and physics. However, he could not financially afford to finish his degree. Despite this, Galileo did not stop learning. He continued to study mathematics and moving objects, teaching some classes in order to pay the bills. Slowly, his fame as an author and professor began to grow. Galileo supported Copernicus' heliocentric theory that the sun is the center of the solar system, and all of the planets revolve around the sun. This went against the Catholic Church and Aristotle's ideas.

In 1609, Galileo heard about a telescope made by a Dutch eyeglasses manufacturer. He improved upon the design, and pointed his telescope skyward. The next year he published <u>The Starry Messenger</u>. In this book he told of his findings that the moon was not a perfect silver circle, but a sphere with mountains and craters. Galileo saw the phases of Venus, like the phases of the moon. This proved that Venus went around the sun, not the Earth. He discovered the four largest moons of Jupiter, revolving around Jupiter. They still bear his name of Galilean Satellites. He also saw sunspots, which refuted the long held belief that the sun was perfect. Although all of these findings went against the ancient teachings of Aristotle, Galileo insisted that they did not contradict the Bible. He studied extensively, and found nothing in Scriptures to contradict his scientific findings. Nevertheless, the Catholic church ordered Galileo cease his research and not to teach the Copernican theory.

When there was a turnover in the papacy, Galileo was allowed to continue to study and publish on the condition that he never mentioned the Copernican theory. However Galileo published a book supporting the heliocentric theory. After an extensive trial, he was convicted of heresy and spent the rest of his life under house arrest. Galileo had three children whom he loved, but possibly for financial or social reasons he never married their mother. Galileo died in 1642. His achievements earned him the title, "The Father of Modern Science."

("Galileo Galilei." Bio. A&E Television Networks, 2014. Web. 17 Dec. 2014.)

HERO OF ALEXANDRIA

Hero (also called Heron) of Alexandria was a Greek mathematician. He was born in about 10 AD in Roman-occupied Egypt. He taught at the Museum in Alexandria. He studied theoretical math (like geometry, arithmetic, astronomy and physics), and manual math (like metallurgy, architecture, and carpentry). He invented numerous machines and wrote many books.

In his book, <u>Pneumatica</u>, Heron described the theoretical pressure in fluids and explained an assortment of mechanical playthings, "Trick jars that give out wine or water separately or in constant proportions, singing birds and sounding trumpets, puppets that move when a fire is lit on an altar, animals that drink when they are offered water ..."

(A G Drachmann, M S Mahoney, Biography in Dictionary of Scientific Biography (New York 1970-1990).)

Although many scholars discount Heron's genius due to the frivolous nature of his inventions, he used them to make physics relevant to his students. He described over 100 such toys and machines. The following description of his "aeolipile" is perhaps the first steam engine and has many similarities to a jet engine. "The aeolipile was a hollow sphere mounted so that it could turn on a pair of hollow tubes that provided steam to the sphere from a cauldron. The steam escaped from the sphere from one or more bent tubes projecting from its equator, causing the sphere to revolve."

(Biography in Encyclopedia Britannica.)

CAROLUS LINNAEUS

Carolus Linnaeus was born in Sweden in 1707, the first of five children. His father was a Lutheran pastor who loved to work in the garden. Linnaeus was introduced to botany (the study of plants) by his father. Linnaeus' parents wanted him to be a preacher, but he showed no interest and less aptitude. When a local doctor took interest in Linnaeus' fascination with plants, his parents allowed him to pursue his interests. He studied medicine after high school. At this time, medicine was based almost completely on plants. He wrote several impressive papers and books about plants, and became a botany professor. In 1728, Linnaeus explored the plants and people off Lapland. He then explored Sweden's natural resources. Linnaeus realized the need to classify living things. He traveled to the Netherlands, England, Germany, and France to study the living creatures. He began his multi-volume work, <u>Systema Naturae</u>.

He married Sara Lisa Moraea, and they had six children. As a professor, Linnaeus inspired many students.

(Blunt, Wilfrid (2004). Linnaeus: the Compleat Naturalist. London: Frances Lincoln. ISBN 978-0691096360

GEORGE MÜLLER

George Müller was born in 1805 in Prussia, now called Germany. His father was a tax collector. Before he was ten years old, Müller learned where his father kept the government's money, and stole from him regularly. His father wanted Müller to be a clergyman so he could make enough money to take care of his parents in their old age. Müller went to school, but did not take it seriously. One evening when he was fourteen, Müller was out late playing cards with friends, and his mother fell ill and died. He spent the next several days drinking with friends.

Müller went back to school. He learned how to steal from the clergyman. His father had to go away on business when Müller was fifteen. He left George at home to supervise house repairs and study. Müller collected taxes from the villagers who owed his father money, then spent it all on expensive hotels, rich food, and alcohol. This stunt landed him in jail. George doubled his efforts in school, but his tendency toward sin continued. He and his friend, Beta, went on a 43 day frolic to Switzerland. When they got home, Beta felt terrible about their decisions, so started meeting with a Christian group. Müller tagged along and found Christ.

At age 20, Jesus turned Müller's life around. He got a job helping American professors learn German. He began preaching and lived at an orphanage. Müller felt called to mission work among Jewish people. He did a Bible study every morning and held prayer meetings every evening. He met and married Mary Groves, a Christian woman. They decided to depend on God to meet ALL of their needs. No matter how urgent a need was, their strategy was prayer. They did not ask other people, they prayed to God to provide, and whatever they needed always came: money, food, healing, shelter. They settled in Bristol, England and began the "Scriptural Knowledge Institution for Home and Abroad." The objectives were to distribute Bibles and spread the Word among all people of all languages. The Orphan House was Müller's most famous work.

Müller built many orphanages and never went into debt. He was divinely given seven and a half million dollars over his life, and kept none for himself. Over three thousand children came to know Christ because of Müller's ministry. He died in 1898 in his room at Orphan House Number Three, having preached his last sermon three days prior. His life is an inspiration to Christians through the ages.

(Reese, Edward. The Life and Ministry of George Müller: Christian Hall of Fame Series. Fundamental Publishers, 1975. ASIN: B0006YDHPU)

ISAAC NEWTON

Isaac Newton was born in Woolsthorpe, England on Jan 4, 1643. He was a premature baby, so small and weak he was not expected to live. His father died before he was born, and his mother left him to live with his grandmother from age 3-12. She wanted him to be a farmer, like his father. But Newton was terrible at this work, so she sent him to school. To support himself he worked as a waiter and cleaned the rooms of wealthier students. The Scientific Revolution was in progress, and people were becoming accustomed to the heliocentric view of the universe (the sun is the center). Newton was so fascinated with advanced science that he did not do good work in his standard classes. He graduated with no honors or distinctions.

While spending time at Cambridge to further his education in 1665, the Great Plague struck Europe. Cambridge sent all of the students home. During this "vacation" Newton developed infinitesimal calculus, developed his theories of light and color, and came to understand planetary motion. When the Great Plague subsided, Newton went on to successfully research and publish. He investigated many of the principles still accepted in modern physics. His most famous work was Philosophiae Naturalis Principia Mathematica. It is, perhaps, the most influential book of all science. In the height of his fame he said, "If I have seen further than others, it is by standing upon the shoulders of giants." The giants refer to the scientists who went before him.

He never married and had very few friends. Most of his life was wrought with conflict and anxiety. But he was one of the smartest physicists of all time. At the end of his life when he was asked how he assessed his achievements, he replied, "I do not know what I may appear to the world; but to myself I seem to have been only like a boy playing on the seashore, and diverting myself now and then in finding a smoother pebble or prettier shell than ordinary, while the great ocean of truth lay all undiscovered before me." He died in London, England on March 31, 1727.

("Sir Isaac Newton." Bio. A&E Television Networks, 2014. Web. 04 Dec. 2014.)

LEONARDO DA VINCI

Leonardo da Vinci was born in Tuscany in 1452. His father was an attorney while his mother was a peasant. His parents never married, and they had a total of 17 children (da Vinci's half siblings) with other people. His father and uncle were interested in his artistic talent and thus encouraged him. He was mostly self-educated, with little formal schooling. But he loved learning and was a "Renaissance man" in that he studied painting, architecture, science, nature, anatomy, weaponry, as well as art. Da Vinci did not view science, art, and nature as separate subjects, but as connected concepts. Although he did not produce vast amounts of art work, his paintings are among the most famous in the world, such as the *Mona Lisa* and *The Last Supper*.

Da Vinci kept extensive notebooks of his ideas and inventions. In order to keep his ideas secret, da Vinci wrote some of his notebooks in left-handed mirror script. In these notebooks are drawings of bicycles, airplanes, submarines, military tanks, and helicopters. It is thought that he only drew most of these contraptions, and did not actually create working models. History does not tell us that da Vinci ever married or had children. Da Vinci died in France in 1591. His exact gravesite is unknown.

("Leonardo da Vinci." 2009. History.com. A&E Networks. 10 Dec. 2014)

LYNN TOWNSEND WHITE, JR

Lynn Townsend White, Jr. was born in 1907 in San Francisco, California. His father was a Presbyterian minister. He followed his father into ministry and earned many academic accolades. He received a prestigious education at Stanford and then taught at Princeton before returning to teach at Stanford. He then became president of Mills College, a school for women. He wrote a book called Educating Our Daughters which pointed to the obstacles women faced in order to obtain a higher education. White then joined the history faculty of the University of California in Los Angeles, where he remained until retirement.

(Bert S. Hall. Lynn Townsend White Jr. Technology and Culture, Vol. 30. No. 1, Jan 1989)

White was very interested in technology from the medieval ages, like the stirrup, wind mill, wheeled plough, wheel barrow, and hand mill (Lynn White, "Technology and Invention in the Middle Ages", Speculum, Vol. 15, No. 2, Apr., 1940). His most influential work was, Medieval Technology and Social Change. It was an overview of medieval technology from Asia and Europe. White lived in the aftermath of the Industrial Revolution, which led him to consider how humans treated the planet. White realized that many natural resources were limited. He concluded that medieval Christians thought they were to dominate nature. This mindset, which had continued through the ages, was damaging the planet. (Technology and Invention in the Middle Ages, Vol. 15, [1940]: 141-59). White said, "we stand amid the debris of our inherited religious system"

(Lynn White, Jr., "Christian Myth and Christian History", Journal of the History of Ideas, Vol. 3, No. 2, Apr. 1942).

Although White was a Christian, his ideas were met with much opposition from the Christian community. But Medieval Technology and Social Change is still an influential work. White challenged Christians to think about the history of environmental problems. He asked them to rethink dominion over the Earth. White taught humility and responsibility. White died in 1987.

(Don Marietta, Jr., "Environmental Philosophy is Environmental Activism: The Most Radical and Effective Kind", Environmental Philosophy and Environmental Activism, Rowman and Littlefield, 1995)

BIG BIBLE SCIENCE

Christian Focus Publications publishes books for adults and children under its four main imprints: Christian Focus, CF4K, Mentor and Christian Heritage.

CHRISTIAN FOCUS PUBLICATIONS

f Christian Focus   **H** Christian Heritage   **K** CF4K   **M** Mentor

Our books reflect our conviction that God's Word is reliable and Jesus is the way to know him, and live forever with him.

Our children's publication list includes a Sunday School curriculum that covers pre-school to early teens, and puzzle and activity books. We also publish personal and family devotional titles, biographies and inspirational stories that children will love.

If you are looking for quality Bible teaching for children then we have an excellent range of Bible stories and age-specific theological books.

From pre-school board books to teenage apologetics, we have it covered!

Find us at our web page: www.christianfocus.com